SINGLE AND PREGNANT

Single and Pregnant

by Ruth I. Pierce

Beacon Press   Boston

For K.F.B.

and problems

Acknowledgments

In preparing the Acknowledgments I suggested making a long list of members of my family, my friends, my clients, and a number of Significant Others who have contributed to this book. The list is indeed a long one, and it is my nature to want to thank everyone personally, partly because a number of people do not even realize in what ways they have helped or influenced me. But Mary did not say very much when I suggested making a long list of names, and I have learned to ponder the point when Mary greets my suggestions with silence.

And so, to be specific, I would like to thank my colleagues at the Florence Crittenton Home in San Francisco who have continually tried to understand and respond to the needs and problems of the single, pregnant girl in a rapidly changing society. I am especially indebted to Jean Bolton May, Natalia Neil, and Helen Thompson. I would also like to thank Dr. Karl Hanson, consulting psychiatrist on the staff, for his many insights as well as for guiding me to Beacon Press.

Many of my impressions regarding medical care and hospital practices evolved out of meetings with staff members at the University of California Medical Center. Marna Cohen and Sally Loos offered a great deal of helpful information. In these meetings the nursing staff was extremely tolerant of us social workers and our idiosyncratic ways of doing things. I am especially indebted to Irene Coleman for suggesting and making it possible for me to be present during a delivery so that I could observe and appreciate the live drama of childbirth.

In researching for the book I found a number of sources especially helpful. These include Lawrence Lader's book *Abortion* and a variety of articles and papers issued through the local Association to Repeal Abortion Laws, which owes its success and renown to Patricia Maginnis. I am grateful to the National Clergy Consultation Service on Abortion for helpful comments and permission to publish their phone numbers. I have relied heavily on material from *Pregnancy and Birth* by Alan Guttmacher, M.D., for specific information about pregnancy. *Adopting a Child Today* by Rael Jean Isaac offered a fresh and useful perspective on adoption; and Jeanne Olander's study called *The Single Parent and Her Baby . . . implications for community action* was extremely helpful in pointing out the problems of and general lack of services to the single mother. The 1966 directory of *Maternity Homes and Residential Facilities for Unmarried Mothers* published by the National Council on Illegitimacy provided me with the data for evolving a profile of maternity homes as they exist today.

The inspiration to write this book came from attending a particular group meeting of parents, pregnant daughters, and several of their boyfriends. This book is the outcome of the concerns and questions that were expressed over a period of time by many parents and girls and by a few boyfriends of single pregnant girls. All of the girls I worked with contributed in one way or another to my appreciation of pregnancy as a rather common occurrence among single women, with rather stiff penalties—socially, financially, and emotionally.

Without listing them, I thank the members of my family and many, many friends for their suggestions and encouragement throughout the preparation of this manuscript.

All three of my typists would qualify for marathon competitions: Mrs. Ruth Halley, Mary Hardy, and Ellen Richards. I thank them all for their dedication, accuracy, and endurance.

I express special appreciation to Fred Berman, M.D., for his sensitive and careful reading of the manuscript which yielded a number of constructive changes. Not only did he serve as an expert on medical questions, but he also appreciated and anticipated many other concerns a reader might have.

And finally, I wish to thank Mary Morris, my editor, who in a skillful and subtle way persuaded me that I could make changes in the manuscript which I never thought I would agree to and that I could meet deadlines, too. I am both pleased and relieved with the outcome.

R. I. Pierce

Berkeley, California
April 1970

Contents

xi

Contents xii

Introduction

No solution to being single and pregnant is straight and simple. Marriage may save you from being single, but you will still be pregnant. Abortion eliminates the problem, but obtaining one is often difficult and expensive. Having the baby and giving him up for adoption is not especially easy. On the other hand, by keeping him you assume a whole new set of responsibilities when you enter the world of the single parent.

An unwed pregnancy is still considered a scandal in this country. A family goes to great pain and expense to conceal a pregnant daughter from relatives and neighbors. Consequently relatives and neighbors have to conceal their pregnant daughters too. The need for secrecy prevents an exchange of information about ways the crisis can be handled. At the same time, families fail to complain about inadequate services because they do not want to attract attention. Therefore, there is little incentive to improve existing services, leaving girls at the mercy of whomever they can find to help them.

A pregnant girl requires a variety of services, which are rarely advertised. Nor are they available though a single source. For example, if she wants to find out about getting an abortion, she often has to go "underground" to get information. If she wants a place to stay during her pregnancy, she may be referred to a maternity home. She may need a social worker from an adoption agency to help her plan for the baby, and she may also have to apply to the Welfare Department for financial assistance. In the meantime, she receives medical care at a hospital or clinic. At each agency or organization, she has to keep repeating her story, and finally she finds herself involved with so many different doctors and social workers that she has no idea whom she can depend on for what.

Most professional people as well as laymen are influenced by unfortunate and inaccurate stereotypes of the "unwed mother." Referring to a young girl or to a grown woman as an "unwed" or an "unmarried mother" simply serves to perpetuate these stereotypes. For the purposes of this book, let us call her instead a "single, pregnant woman." Then she at least sounds independent and adult, as compared with an "unmarried" and therefore presumably *unwanted* mother (which she never actually becomes until after the baby is born).

Pregnancy occurs in women of all ages and sizes, backgrounds and interests, regardless of marital status. Logically it follows that women will differ in what they decide to do about the situation. You may feel that a pregnancy at this time in your life is the worst possible thing that could happen to you, but this is not necessarily true for everyone. Some girls may be secretly or even openly pleased about the whole thing, and look forward to having the baby. For some girls the pregnancy may be just the touch they need to precipitate marriage, or the push to move away from home at last. As the reactions vary, so do the choices and the decisions.

The purpose of this book is to tell you about the alternatives that may be available so that you can think about what you want to do and make choices instead of drifting along the path of least resistance. Some girls will want an abortion, and that is all there is to it. To others, the thought alone may be highly offensive. Each of you will have to find what suits you best. If a course of action seems foolish or wrong to you, remember that, at least for the time being, no single solution will be acceptable to everyone, and each of you has to do the best you can within the limitations of our present system.

As the book proceeds, you will see that many of the alternatives require early planning. Since services are limited and are usually offered on a first-come first-serve basis, the earlier you get started the more choices you have. Requests for service can *always* be canceled, but you can never be sure of getting what you need if you wait until the last minute.

You will have to make some big decisions in the next few months, and you will need some help. But try not to let anyone make your decisions for you. It may seem tough at the time, but being pregnant is *your* experience, involving *your* body, and *your* emotions. It is *your* baby who is involved and *your* future.

SINGLE AND PREGNANT

CHAPTER ONE

Avoiding pregnancy: the basic facts

In spite of the abundance of concern and discussion *about* sex, it can still be difficult for a single girl to obtain the information she needs to avoid becoming pregnant. Furthermore, information alone is not always enough; if a woman engages in sexual relations, some form of birth control must be used to reduce the risk of her becoming pregnant, unless she wants to be.

At this point let us consider what is required for a pregnancy to begin and some of the ways for preventing it. A woman can only become pregnant if sperm from a man's penis enter her body by way of the opening called the vagina. Presumably you know that impregnation occurs when sperm from the man surrounds and penetrates an egg, which is located inside the woman's body.

A woman's orgasm has nothing to do with whether or not she becomes pregnant. However, you have probably noticed a secretion when you are sexually aroused. This mucous fluid lubricates the woman's vaginal area, so that it is easier for the man to get his penis inside her. This substance is also the perfect environment for sperm to swim in so that they quickly and easily reach the cervical canal. *Biologically your body is designed to become pregnant if nothing is done to stop it.*

I

Although it is unusual, girls have become pregnant when intercourse did not occur, but sperm managed to get into their vagina. This can happen in several ways. For example, if you have anal intercourse it is possible that sperm might travel back out of the rectum into the vaginal area, or after oral intercourse sperm can unintentionally be carried back down to the vaginal area by hand or mouth.

Theoretically the sperm can only reach the egg at a certain time in a woman's monthly cycle, so it is particularly important either to avoid intercourse at this time of the month or to use some method for preventing the sperm from getting to the egg.

The Rhythm Method

Many people dabble with home-style interpretations of the rhythm method. According to the rhythm method, you should not have intercourse during a special time of the month; the problem lies in accurately figuring out when this "special time" (called ovulation) occurs for *you*. In order to do this with *any* hope of success, you have to start out by keeping a careful record of your menstrual periods for at least a year. Even if you do work out a pattern of fertile and nonfertile days, it is awkward to confine a sexual relationship to this kind of schedule, and there is still no guarantee that you will not become pregnant.

Pregnancy may occur for several reasons. First of all, the time of ovulation varies from woman to woman, from month to month. It shifts as a result of a great number of things, such as a change of routine, climate, diet, emotional trauma, illness, or hormonal balance. Many women, after depending on a regular cycle for years, suddenly find themselves unexpectedly pregnant. Younger girls who are still growing and changing are often irregular in their ovulation patterns. For them the rhythm method is entirely unreliable. Narcotics can alter a woman's ovluation pattern so that she menstruates irregularly, leaving her with no way of knowing if she might be pregnant. Although it is unusual, girls have conceived as a result of intercourse during their menstrual periods, the one time in the month they were *sure* they were safe. In other words, the rhythm method often fails because *no* time in the month is ever one hundred percent safe for anybody all of the time.

Withdrawal

People usually realize that the rhythm method does not work very well, so instead they may use a method called withdrawal. The man removes his penis from the woman's vagina immediately before he has an orgasm. This method *does not work* because, as many people do not realize, sperm and seminal fluid are secreted from the end of the penis long before the moment of orgasm. Sometimes during love-play before intercourse, you will notice drops of fluid on the end of the man's penis. It is amazing how many men think those drops are a lubricant that does not contain any sperm. However, that fluid is *loaded* with sperm, perhaps the most active of all! And more sperm are likely to follow throughout intercourse, long before the man reaches orgasm and actually ejaculates. So if a man waits to withdraw until the last minute, it is probably too late, and already thousands of sperm have been released into the woman's vaginal area.

Douching

For many years people have believed that douching, washing out the woman's genital area immediately after intercourse, prevents pregnancy. It sounds reasonable, but douching is not effective. Sperm move so quickly and directly that some of them reach the cervical canal way up inside the woman's body within thirty seconds. By the time she has grabbed her douche bag and filled it with warm water, it is already much too late. Sometimes the jet of water will actually encourage the sperm upward. Douching might wash out some of the sperm, but it can never wash out all of them. Women have douched with a variety of mixtures, including Coca-Cola. These are intended to deactivate the sperm or to kill them altogether. Some of the methods people use are very dangerous. In the meantime, they are ineffective because they cannot be administered fast enough.

When you combine the information that has been presented so far, it seems highly risky to have intercourse without additional protection. This is complicated because, for one thing, it means that you have to *plan* in advance. If you feel uncomfortable about having sexual relations because you are not married, naturally you feel self-conscious about going to a pharmacist or to a doctor and asking for birth control. Many boys are also embarrassed and self-conscious about going into a drugstore and buying contraceptives. What you have to remember is that brief encounters with a druggist or a doctor are *nothing* compared to what you will have to go through if you become pregnant.

Another problem that applies to some methods of birth control, and which therefore discourages many women from using them, is the fact that you need access to a bathroom, which may not always be available. This is a significant problem that you have to deal with the best you can.

If a couple does not know each other very well, often they are too shy to bring up the subject of birth control. Many people can engage in sexual relations with one another long before they can discuss what they are doing. Nonetheless, both partners are usually aware of the fact that intercourse can and very well may lead to pregnancy. Since the girl is the one who bears the consequences, the boy will frequently leave it up to her to protect herself. She is foolish if she doesn't.

If you unexpectedly find yourself in a situation that is terribly urgent, and the nearest drugstore is twenty miles away or closed for the night, there are still ways a couple can gratify each other without having the man's penis enter the woman's vagina. The experience may not be as satisfying or rewarding as ordinary intercourse, but if there is any feeling between the two people for each other it is likely that there will be a next time, giving one or the other a chance to prepare for it beforehand. If you suggest alternatives to intercourse in order to avoid getting pregnant, most fellows, even if they pout or protest, will appreciate your concern.

Rubbers and Condoms

Rubbers, or condoms, which are used by the man, are among the devices that can be purchased in a drugstore or supermarket without a prescription. In some states they are available from vending machines in men's rest rooms. Rubbers (also referred to as prophylactics) occasionally come off during intercourse, but generally they are quite effective.

In using this method you must remember that the purpose is to catch *all* of the sperm and to prevent them from entering your body. A rubber is not dependable if, for example, the boy enters your body without a rubber, leaks a little, withdraws, puts on a rubber, and ultimately ejaculates inside the rubber. The rubber caught most of the sperm, but it must catch it all.

The effectiveness of using something like Saran Wrap as a condom depends upon how completely it keeps sperm from entering your body.

If you are entering into a new relationship, condoms are helpful in reducing the risk of catching a venereal disease.

Foams and Jellies

A variety of foams and jellies to be used by the woman are available in drugstores and supermarkets. These substances, which either spray or can be applied with a plastic plunger, contain chemicals which kill the sperm. Foams and jellies must be applied *before* intercourse. Vaginal suppositories work on the same principle. Instructions on the package should be followed very carefully.

The trouble with these methods is that they must be applied almost immediately before intercourse in order to be effective, and they should be used each time you are about to have intercourse. In the meantime, loveplay is a somewhat varied and sensitive business, which can be spoiled by interruptions with mechanical gadgets at the critical moments. Indeed they may be a nuisance (but so is Johnny with his runny nose in the supermarket two years later!). Foams and jellies are better than nothing, but they are not very reliable.

Diaphragm

Some of the more sophisticated devices involve a doctor's prescription. The diaphragm, which was especially popular in days before The Pill, is a round rubber disc with a bendable rubber rim. Diaphragms come in sizes ranging from about the size of a half-dollar to the diameter of a large orange. They bend into a tampon shape, and the woman herself inserts it into the vagina before intercourse. In the meantime, she has doused the diaphragm with jelly to make it easier to insert as well as to increase its efficiency. Once inserted, the diaphragm fans back out into its disc shape and covers the mouth of the cervix, hopefully serving as a dam to block the sperm from going any further into the woman's body. The jelly helps to deactivate the sperm in case a few manage to swim around the rim of the diaphragm. The diaphragm is a reliable method of preventing pregnancy, except that it *must* be used whenever a woman has intercourse, regardless of the time of month and the inconvenience it causes.

You must go to a doctor to be fitted for a diaphragm. Even if you have a friend who wears the same size dress as you, this does not necessarily mean that her diaphragm will fit you. Also, you must learn from the doctor how and when to insert and remove the diaphragm. Any woman who uses a diaphragm should have it checked periodically to make sure it continues to be the right size for her, especially after she has had a baby or if she gains or loses a large amount of weight. She should also check it herself occasionally to make sure that the rubber has not worn through anywhere.

The Intra-Uterine Device (IUD) or Loop

The diaphragm is something you can put in and take out yourself. A more recent and popular device is the IUD or loop (also called the coil) which must be inserted by a doctor. A loop is usually a piece of soft plastic that comes in several different shapes. The doctor uses an instrument to insert it into the uterus through the cervix. It somehow discourages a fertilized egg from attaching itself to the wall of the uterus. The loop can remain in place for years, although it should be checked periodically by a doctor. You should reach up and check occasionally yourself to make sure it is still there.

Women who use the loop may notice heavier and longer menstrual periods as well as a little more cramping than usual. But for some women it is the ideal method. For example, if a woman has been advised against taking birth control pills or if she cannot remember to take pills regularly, she can have a loop inserted and feel reasonably well protected without having to bother with various gadgets each time she has intercourse. Until recently the loop was generally recommended only to women who have already had a child, but new designs have been introduced that are working well for all women.

The perfect birth control device has yet to be invented, but new and better methods are being suggested and tested all the time.

The Pill

Considering all the fuss and bother that goes with most of the methods mentioned so far, you can see why birth control pills became so popular so fast. Not only are they simple and clean, but they are close to one hundred percent effective. A woman rarely becomes pregnant if she is taking one of the many forms of The Pill regularly and faithfully according to instructions. In spite of the present controversy over birth control pills, many women have taken them with no apparent ill effects, and they rejoice at being free of anxiety about becoming pregnant. Others who have taken them have experienced noticeable side effects, such as weight gain, skin eruptions, changes in facial skin color (pregancy masks), irregular periods, and headaches. Sometimes a woman has to try several different kinds of pills before she discovers the brand that produces no side effects for her.

Many doctors maintain that in most cases the physical changes that occur in a woman's body because of The Pill are not as traumatic and dangerous to her life as those that occur when she becomes pregnant. However, some women have medical problems that make it inadvisable for them to take The Pill—*or* to become pregnant! This is one of the reasons it is important to get a prescription from a doctor instead of borrowing an extra packet from a friend. If you have any questions about The Pill, discuss them with your doctor, and read over carefully the printed materials that accompany each packet.

Many women who have been taking The Pill over a long period of time develop a sense of psychological immunity to becoming pregnant. They forget the association between The

Pill they take every morning (or every night) and having intercourse any time they want without worrying about becoming pregnant. The longer a woman takes The Pill, the more confidence she has in the fact that she will not become pregnant. Then all of a sudden, when for one reason or another she stops taking The Pill, she readily becomes pregnant, to her complete and dismal surprise. If you *were* taking The Pill and have stopped, make sure to use some other birth control method.

Sterility and Pregnancy

People make terrible mistakes in assuming that they or their partners are sterile. A common example is the couple who sleep together over a long period of time without using any form of birth control. Since the woman never becomes pregnant, they both begin to forget about the relationship between intercourse and pregnancy. Sometimes the woman does become pregnant eventually. In other cases she does not become pregnant by that particular man but by someone else later on because she did not think it was necessary to protect herself.

Girls who have had one ovary and tube removed often expect that they will have trouble becoming pregnant. Even though it seems logical that they would be less fertile with one ovary removed, the other ovary usually does the work of two and the woman still ovulates every month. In most cases she is just as likely to become pregnant after the operation as she was before.

Some fellows will try to persuade you that they are sterile, but they do not always know what they are talking about. One young man seriously believed he was sterile because he had had mumps. Unfortunately, his girl friend also believed him and had a baby. Another girl complained that she became pregnant by a man who had surgery to make him sterile (a vasectomy). Usually these operations are reliable.

Some men may insist that they are sterile because they have never used contraceptives and they have never made a woman pregnant. If the fellow is married it may be that his wife is sterile, not he. If he is single he may not have kept very close track of all the girls he has had relations with. Childlessness in itself is not conclusive proof of sterility. Fathering children is important enough to most men, so that if they have failed to have children within a marriage, they may need to test their abilities elsewhere.

CHAPTER TWO

Diagnosis

MORNING-AFTER TREATMENT

If you have had intercourse without any protection at all there is a fair chance that you may be pregnant. If you think that you *might* be pregnant but do not want to sit around and wait to find out, you may want to consider what is called the Morning-After Treatment (although it is subject to some of the same questions that are currently being raised about The Pill). This treatment must be administered within forty-eight hours from the time you had intercourse, so you cannot afford to delay for a moment. The treatment, offered in the form of pills, is a large dose of hormone, which by temporarily altering the lining the uterus, prevents a fertilized egg from attaching itself. You will probably be given diethylstilbestrol, a synthetic estrogen, which may cause you to feel nauseated and uncomfortable for a few days. The treatment costs about twenty dollars, but it is worth it if it spares you further anxiety about being pregnant. This is in no way recommended as an everyday method for avoiding pregnancy, but it is effective in an emergency.

The Morning-After Treatment *must* be prescribed by a physician, so you cannot expect to obtain it from a pharmacist. Also it is still very new and controversial, so it may not be available everywhere. If you live in a big city, call the local

11

Planned Parenthood office. If they do not offer the Morning-After Treatment ask if they can refer you to a doctor who does. You can also call the local Medical Society and ask for a list of doctors who specialize in obstetrics and gynecology (Ob–Gyn). When you call a doctor's office make sure he offers the treatment before you go in for an appointment. Otherwise you might find yourself paying fifteen to twenty dollars for a lecture on morals.

If you live in a smaller city that does not have a Planned Parenthood office, and services do not seem to be immediately available, do not hesitate to make a few long distance calls to the nearest large city to find out where you can get help. (Often people pay more attention to long distance calls.) If you are worried about gossip in a small-town community, you may want to seek outside help anyway. Depending on where you live and what your schedule is, you may not be able to get the Morning-After Treatment in time for it to be effective. If this is the case, all you can do is to pray, be patient, and maybe your period will come on schedule. In the meantime, make sure you are prepared and have *something* on hand to use when you have intercourse next time.

Many people are confusing the Morning-After Treatment with shots that can be given to bring on a delayed menstrual period. There is a tremendous difference between these two treatments. The Morning-After pills will probably cancel the effects of having had intercourse without protection and you will not become pregnant. The shots that are given to bring on a delayed menstrual period do *only* that! They will bring on your period *only* if your period is late and you are not pregnant. If you are pregnant, these shots will not do anything to change the situation.

EARLY SYMPTOMS OF PREGNANCY

By now you realize that you cannot be pregnant unless you have had intercourse or have participated in sexual activity that has resulted in the release of sperm by a man in the area of your genitals.

Now let us say that you have had intercourse and you are worried that you might be pregnant. Either it is too late for the Morning-After Treatment, or it is unavailable to you. The first suspicious symptom of pregnancy is missing a menstrual period. Many girls become so upset and anxious that they miscount the days and assume that their periods are late when they are not even due for another week. Others do not keep track of their cycles, and do not know for sure when to expect their next periods. Others become so fearful of being pregnant that the emotional stress alone causes their periods to be late. Narcotics definitely interfere with a woman's normal menstrual pattern. If your periods are irregular for any reason it is difficult to know if you are pregnant or not. The days of waiting and wondering can be frightening, especially if you have no idea what you are going to do if it turns out that you are pregnant.

Sometimes if a girl has experienced the panic of waiting for her period, she is enormously relieved when it finally comes. But then almost instantly she forgets what the anxiety was all about, and before you know it, she is having sexual relations again without any protection. Eventually she will become pregnant unless she does something to avoid it. Having an appointment scheduled to get birth control is not enough. Every time you have intercourse you are taking a significant chance of becoming pregnant unless you use some kind of precaution.

Some pregnant women bleed very slightly and for only a day or two at the time the next period is due. If you are worried about being pregnant, you may be too eager to accept a scant discharge as your scheduled period, even though you know it is different from your regular periods. It is not unusual for a girl to have slight periods during the first couple of months of pregnancy, but the difference between a regular period and a period after the beginning of a pregnancy is *usually* obvious enough so that you notice it.

You may begin to notice other symptoms of pregnancy shortly after the time when your period was due. You may feel nauseated when you wake up in the morning or at some other time of the day. Some women feel queasy; others actually vomit daily, which can be awkward, especially if you cannot always depend on privacy in the rest room. You may also find yourself sensitive to certain tastes or smells that never especially bothered you before.

Another common symptom of early pregnancy (which could also be caused by other things) is a need to urinate more often than usual. You may also find that you are tired and lethargic, as if you can never get enough sleep. You may notice a loss of appetite. During the first few weeks you may even lose a few pounds, all the while thinking that if you were pregnant you would be gaining weight.

Some women know intuitively as soon as they are pregnant. Others have no symptoms or suspicions whatever until several months have gone by. These women have slight menstrual periods, enough to satisfy them, and otherwise they feel fine. Some women, of course, feel miserable from the first day.

PREGNANCY TESTS

You may be pretty well convinced that you are pregnant, but it is a good idea to have a pregnancy test anyway. This may be the most difficult step to take. Thus far perhaps you have been trying to conceal the symptoms, even from yourself, wishing and hoping that by some stroke of luck they will go away. In the meantime you realize that once you go in for a test you have to face a number of troublesome questions: First of all, what if you are pregnant? Once you are sure, then what? Also, what is the doctor going to think of you when you present yourself for the test? Once he knows, who else is going to find out?

It is this period of suspense and indecision that can be the most lonely and frightening. However, once you know for sure, you can begin to *do* something instead of simply panicking every time the thought crosses your mind.

If you are young and living at home, you may eventually have to tell your parents that you suspect you are pregnant. You may even *want* to tell your parents. Your mother may have guessed. Often a girl is afraid to tell her parents; in the meantime her parents suspect, but they do not want to accuse their daughter. So nobody says anything for several months until a tummy begins to protrude, and finally somebody has to say something.

If your mother knows, it would be nice if she could call and make an appointment for you to go in and have a pregnancy test. On the other hand, if your mother goes to pieces, or you decide not to tell your parents, you will have to call and make the appointment yourself. Sometimes it is easier if you can find a friend to go along with you. Or maybe your boyfriend will go. Sometimes a friend's parents can be much more helpful than your own parents during the early stages of finding out if you are pregnant and deciding what to do.

Recently in California a law was passed which permits minors to seek medical care without the permission of their parents. Other states may eventually put such laws into effect, but until then, if you are a minor, ask how old you have to be to have the test without your parents' signed consent. This may also depend on the clinic or the doctor. For information about having a pregnancy test you can call the following:

Planned Parenthood
Public health department
County hospital
Doctors of obstetrics and gynecology (the Yellow Pages should have a fairly accurate listing)
Some college health centers (word generally gets around quickly if a health center is conservative and moralistic or relaxed and helpful regarding pregnancy among the students)

Pregnancy tests run anywhere from five to twenty dollars. Most clinics probably charge less than a private doctor. The earliest you can have the test and hope for reliable and conclusive results is a few days after the day you expected your period. When you make the appointment, you will probably be asked to bring in a urine sample. Various kinds of medication, even including large amounts of aspirin, may cause the test to appear positive when it is actually negative, so if you have taken anything be sure to mention it to the person who is administering the test. Usually you can find out the results within a few hours.

Sometimes a urine test is all that is needed to indicate whether you are pregnant. However, depending on the circumstances and how advanced you are in the pregnancy, a doctor may decide to give you a pelvic examination. Women are often apprehensive about having such an examination, especially if they have never had one before. The doctor has an examining table with stirrup-like footrests at one end. The patient lies on her back with her knees spread and pointed upwards; her lower half is covered with a sheet. If you tell the doctor that you are frightened or that you have never been examined before, he or she may try even harder to be as gentle as possible with you. He may tell you what he is going to do as he proceeds so that you will not be so tense and afraid.

The doctor explores your pelvic area with the fingers of one hand inside you, the other hand probing and testing from the abdomen on the outside. Even in early pregnancy, the uterus begins to feel soft and enlarged; sometimes the doctor can diagnose your condition from his examination. (Occasionally the symptoms you thought were early signs of pregnancy are indicative of a cyst or some other condition.) If a doctor is gentle, the examination should not be especially painful. Probably the undignified posture bothers most women more than anything else. If you are worried or fearful about having a pelvic exam, mention this when you call to make the initial appointment. Some women are more comfortable if they are examined by a lady doctor. Do not be shy about asking if one is available.

Usually if the results of the examination are positive it means that you are pregnant, and it is unlikely that there has been a mistake.

If the tests are negative, you can breathe a sigh of relief. However, it is a good idea to go back for a second test if you miss a second period. Unfortunately doctors do make mistakes and occasionally laboratory results come out negative the first time. If you have any reason to continue suspecting that you are pregnant, it is a good idea to have a second test.

If you are not pregnant, stop for a moment and think about what you are doing. During a pregnancy scare many girls promise themselves that they will never have relations again until they are safely married. But these promises are not very realistic. Besides, by the time you are married you should be familiar with ways of protecting yourself so that you are pregnant only when you want to be.

Ask about birth control at the clinic or hospital where you have your pregnancy test. Sometimes doctors and other staff members are not allowed to recommend birth control unless the patient brings up the subject herself and asks for information. This may also be true for abortion referrals.

If you *are* pregnant then you have other things to think about. Some girls instantly desire an abortion. Others are utterly bewildered and have no idea what to do. If the doctor or nurse who delivers the news is sensitive and caring, he or she may help you to work out a plan for the next few days or weeks. The doctor may have his nurse call and make an appointment for you with an agency or counseling person who specializes in this type of situation.

If you express interest in an abortion, the doctor may advise you on the procedures for requesting a therapeutic abortion in your state. He might even make appointments for you to see the necessary people to approve such an operation. However, in most states therapeutic abortions are still allowed only in order to save the life of the mother. If that is the case, the doctor may discreetly advise you on where to get an illegal abortion.

You may find the doctor and his staff very sympathetic and kind. On the other hand, they may be detached and disinterested, leaving you totally alone and heavy with your problem. Instead of allowing yourself to become discouraged, turn quickly to some other source for direction and support.

WHEN IS YOUR BABY DUE?

If you are pregnant, two dates become very important as you anticipate what you are going to do. One of these is the date of your last menstrual period (abbreviated LMP). This refers to the *first* day of your last normal menstrual period, and it is the crucial key in predicting how pregnant you are and on what date your baby is due. The due date is referred to as "estimated date of confinement," abbreviated EDC. The date on which you had intercourse is not especially helpful, since the duration of pregnancy is determined according to your menstrual cycle. From now on, many of the people you contact for help or service will immediately ask you for the date of your last menstrual period. This is so they can figure out according to their own method either how pregnant you are or approximately when your baby is due. You may say you are two months pregnant, but the person questioning you is not sure you are figuring the same way he or she is.

Some girls do not keep track of their periods, or they cannot remember, or they are terribly irregular, or they had one of those scant periods which may or may not have been normal. Sometimes you have to guess about when you had your last period. (As the pregnancy advances, doctors can often begin to tell how pregnant you are by feeling the size and position of your uterus.)

To determine your EDC, the approximate date your baby will be born, you can use several formulas, but this seems to be the easiest one: Starting with the date of the first day of your last menstrual period, subtract three from the month and add seven to the day. Let us say that the first day of your last menstrual period was July 10. Subtract three months from July which gives you April, and add seven days to the 10, which is 17. Your EDC would be April 17.

EDC's are very nebulous dates. They give you a general indication of when you might expect your baby, plus or minus a few days, or even weeks. A normal pregnancy for a human being in good health lasts for approximately 280 days, or 40 weeks from the first day of the last normal menstrual period. If you were not able to follow the formula, you can count 40 weeks off on a calendar.

POSSIBILITY OF MISCARRIAGE

If you are pregnant and you do not know what to do, a fairly common response is to ignore the whole thing, hoping that somehow it will go away. This *may* happen, but you cannot count on it. Sometimes girls miscarry. Some doctors say that the chances are one in ten. Others say the chances are even greater. Miscarriages usually occur within the first three months of the pregnancy. After that it becomes less and less likely with every week that goes by. If you are young and became pregnant with very little sexual experience, and if you have never had a miscarriage, you will probably carry this baby to term.

Perhaps you have heard about false pregnancies: a woman reacts and expands as if she were pregnant but she has no baby inside of her. This is a rather rare phenomenon and it is not a very reliable fantasy to hang your hopes on as a way out of your situation.

ADVANTAGES OF EARLY DIAGNOSIS

You will have certain advantages if you are able to admit to yourself that you are pregnant before you actually begin to "show." For example, if you decide to get married, you have some time to work things out with your boyfriend and to make arrangements for the wedding without having to look for your wedding dress in a maternity shop.

If you decide to get an abortion, you have time to locate a responsible person to do the operation. The more pregnant you are, the more dangerous an abortion becomes, and usually the cost goes up accordingly. In California, where more and more abortions are being performed legally, there is still a twenty-week limit from the first day of your last menstrual period, after which doctors may not legally perform the operation. In New York the limit is twenty-four weeks. Refer to Chapter Six for more complete information on abortions.

If neither marriage nor abortion is the solution to your problem it is still important to be thinking about what you are going to do. If you might be interested in going to a maternity home, call and inquire about their services. Most of them take reservations and have long waiting lists. Nothing is more bewildering than calling a maternity home at the last minute to find that it is filled, leaving you with no other place to go. Do not worry if your plans change somewhere along the way, and you decide you do not want to go. You can always cancel your reservation, and somebody else will be grateful to take your place.

The same principle applies to adoption service. Many girls think that plenty of families are eager to adopt babies, but this is not always true. Many agencies accept only as many babies as they can definitely place. If you wait until the last minute, the agency may have already accepted its quota, leaving you with a baby in your arms and no place to put him. If, on the other hand, you do reserve a place for your baby in an adoption agency, and later on you change your mind, you can always cancel your application, again opening a space for someone else.

When you are pregnant, your health is extremely important. Some women have no trouble at all, but others must be carefully supervised for proper diet, exercise, and other aspects of health care. Whether you plan to keep your baby or to give him up for adoption, you want him to arrive as healthy and strong as possible. If you are planning to keep him, nothing is more disheartening and exhausting than caring for a sickly baby, especially if you are all by yourself. If, on the other hand, you plan to give the baby up, an agency or a family will be reluctant to accept him if he is not in perfect health. It is therefore a good idea to sign up for prenatal care with a physician or clinic early in pregnancy. Although your prenatal visits at the doctor's office may be uneventful, at least a doctor has a chance to follow your progress through the pregnancy, and he is available if at any moment something begins to go wrong.

Finally, at some point you are going to have to deal with a change in your shape. If you decide to move or change jobs, you will feel more confident in applying as a tenant or employee when you are still trim. Once that bulge begins to emerge about your middle, you will have to deal with the skeptical looks of landlords and personnel managers, and if you are self-conscious and uncomfortable about the situation, it will not be easy. Girls, in spite of their best intentions, often get stuck during the final months of a pregnancy with no savings, no place to stay, and no job. In the meantime, the maternity homes in the area are filled and the adoption agencies have refused their applications. Suddenly, there you are, big as life, and what on earth are you supposed to do now?

CHAPTER THREE

Boyfriends and parents

Hoping that you have not yet reached the desperate quandary described at the end of the last chapter, let's go back to the point at which you have just discovered that you are pregnant. The circumstances are so entirely different for every woman that it is impossible to prescribe a solution that will work equally well for everyone. Also, circumstances can change during a pregnancy, and what seemed like a good solution in the early months may be no longer relevant by the time the baby is born. Bear this in mind as you consider the choices you have and decide what plan is best for you.

In becoming pregnant you have acquired a great deal of responsibility, which may at times seem like more than you can handle. However, you must remember that this is *your* pregnancy and *your* baby. In order to maintain control over your own decisions, you will have to choose carefully whom to tell, at least at the beginning. What you need is moral support and concrete guidance. What you do *not* need is to find yourself surrounded by people who are panicky and upset. This could apply to the baby's father, your parents, your employer, your grandmother, or to any number of other people who might eventually become involved.

BOYFRIENDS

Who are some of the key people who might be helpful? One of the most logical people to contact, of course, is the father himself. On the other hand, he may be the *last* person in the world you want to go to at this point. For example, you may have just broken up with him, and feel that you never want to see him again, or you may even be involved with someone else by now.

If you are good friends, however, the fellow may be able to offer you emotional support. You may discuss the advantages and disadvantages of getting married under these circumstances. If you both decide that you do not want to get married, he can still participate in the decision about what you are going to do next. Depending on his own attitude and situation, he may be able to help you out financially. (No matter what you do from this point on, either having an abortion or going through a pregnancy and delivering a baby, it is going to cost money, sometimes quite a bit.)

Men are very different in their reactions to the news that they have impregnated a girl. For most the greatest fear is being committed to child-support payments for the next twenty-one years. Some panic instantly and deny that they could in any way be responsible. Others are inwardly rather pleased with themselves, but appear callous for fear of being pressured into assuming responsibility. Still others are angered by the threat of being trapped in a situation that holds no interest or promise for them. Some are utterly delighted and are helpful and responsible. In a large number of cases, the father does not know what he is expected to do, and so he does nothing. Unless the girl pressures him, either on her own or through legal action, he is more or less left to default out of the picture.

Sometimes the partner is simply not available. He may be in the service or off at college or in Europe. Perhaps he is married to someone else, but you may still want him to know you are pregnant. Of course, it can be awkward if you are not sure who of several men might be the father.

Although it is not imperative for you to contact the man involved, sometimes he too can learn from this experience. Often if a man is properly informed about his rights, he is not frightened and can take a more active part in offering support to you and participating in the decisions related to his child. He may also be motivated to be more cautious in the future.

The situation is somewhat different if you are pregnant as the result of rape or an incestuous relationship. Broadly defined, rape is intercourse which occurs between two people who are not married to each other without the mutual consent of both parties. Usually force or some kind of intimidation is involved. Statutory rape, however, occurs when the girl involved is under a certain age which is determined by the laws of each state. In this case the girl or her parents can press charges against the man, and in some states the consequences may be rather severe. This law is intended to protect the innocence of young girls. It is sometimes misused by a girl's parents, who become angry and bitter when they find out that their daughter has been involved in a physical relationship; they want to punish the young man. In some states rape is sufficient grounds for legal abortion.

Incest occurs when close blood relatives have intercourse with each other. This might be brother and sister, mother and son, or father and daughter. Although incest is a criminal offense, few people are ever charged with it, and almost no one is ever convicted. Incest is discouraged as a common practice, partly because of the higher risk that the babies born of such unions will be sickly or deformed. Incest is also sufficient grounds for abortion in some states.

Incest occurs more frequently than many of us realize, but often the girl is afraid to tell anyone. However, if she becomes pregnant as a result, she may be forced to reveal the circumstances and expose the man involved. Hopefully, through some service in the community she will be protected from further assaults or involvements of this kind.

PARENTS

Now what about your parents? Most counselors will advise you to tell your parents, especially if you are under age. They see this as a wonderful opportunity for a family to get to know each other under conditions of stress, and the whole experience will bring you all a lot closer. Sometimes this is true, but it is certainly not universally so. If you are under 21 you may *have* to tell your parents in order to obtain medical care, to gain admission to a maternity home, or in order to sign relinquishment papers for your baby. Some states require parents' signatures on some forms and not on others.

Depending on what state you live in, you may have no choice but to tell at least one of your parents. If both of your parents are ogres, and you are afraid to tell either one of them, maybe some of the suggestions further on in this chapter will be helpful.

Parents react in many different ways, but a daughter's pregnancy is something that most parents do at least react to. Most often they seem to feel terribly guilty; your pregnancy may be an indication that your parents have failed somehow in bringing you up. Or are they really asking, "How could *you* fail *us*?" causing you to feel terribly guilty about abusing their trust. In most cases nobody has really failed anybody. The girl succumbed to her curiosity and her impulses and had intercourse with a boy. Or maybe it was a contraceptive method that failed. At any rate it is human and natural to want to blame *someone* whenever accidents or unexpected events occur. In this case, parents have a choice of blaming you, the boy, or themselves.

Some parents are very much involved with their children and feel responsible for what happens to them. Almost instinctively they know when something is wrong. A girl hates to tell these parents because she does not want to hurt them. And yet she knows it would hurt them even more if she did not tell them and they were to find out later on. Girls often end up telling this kind of parents, who are usually helpful and supportive. Sometimes, a girl may find it impossible to tell her parents the whole truth, if, for example, she is expecting a racially mixed baby. It is as difficult for white girls to tell parents about black boyfriends as it is for black or Oriental girls to confess that the baby will be part Caucasian.

Some parents do not see their children as individuals at all but as extensions of themselves. Whatever happens to their children is a reflection on them. Many of these parents let it be known in subtle ways that they do not want to know about it if their daughter should become pregnant. It is obvious from the way they talk about other girls and their families. If their daughter does tell them, they will be angry with her, mostly for forcing them to deal with a situation which is intolerable for them. Some of these parents may disguise their anger behind a veneer of caring and concern, but underneath they are much more worried about what their friends and neighbors think than they are about what their daughter may be experiencing.

Sometimes girls get pregnant at the worst times, when the whole family is in an uproar. Mother is starting to go through the menopause and anything sets her off in tears. Senile Granny has just moved in, and Sister is getting married next month. How can a girl possibly add to the problems that seem almost too much for the family as it is? Sometimes all of the other crises are not really as important as your family makes them out to be. But if they do seem to be life-and-death issues and you are too young to handle the pregnancy without your parents' help, then you may have to seek help from the outside before you can approach anyone in your family. Sometimes it is much easier for your family to cope with the situation if you have already worked out some of the arrangements for the final months of pregnancy, such as where you are going to stay. Then at least they do not feel that they have to solve another problem when they cannot handle the ones they already have.

Of course each parent is an individual and has his or her way of relating to you and your problems. Parents also have their separate ways of defining and handling crises. Whereas the pregnancy may be unfortunate but understandable to one, it may be total outrage to the other.

It is especially difficult if you are the daughter who has always been held up as an example to the other children in the family. Your parents have placed a heavy responsibility on you to be the "good girl," and you hate to disappoint them. But it is not necessarily fair that you are asked to live out their fantasies of what you *should* be as if you had no integrity and personality of your own.

It is equally awkward if you are the daughter who always seems to get into trouble. Your mother says, "I told you that if you kept seeing that no-good Charlie and coming in every night after midnight . . ." She is right, and yet what can you say? The hour you came home does not have anything to do with it any more. The fact is, you are pregnant and you need help.

When you announce to one or both of your parents that you are pregnant, often you are confronting them with what they perceive as a terrible problem for which they have no solution. How are you going to finish school? Where can they hide you? What about the younger children in the family (and their tendency to tell their friends *everything* . . .)? How much is this going to cost?

When your parents learn that you are pregnant, they may also realize for the first time that you are no longer a child. You may still be very young, but you have participated in an adult act with serious consequences. Parents need time to allow this realization to sink in.

Many parents can be wonderful and understanding until it is time to decide what to do about the pregnancy. Most white, middle-class families favor abortion or adoption, and as long as you are willing to go along with their plan, there is no problem. But what if you decide that you want to have and perhaps keep your baby? All of a sudden parents who are otherwise loving and accepting become resolutely stubborn.

It is inevitable that your parents realize much more fully than you do what it means to bring a baby into the world—to feed it, to provide for it, to love it twenty-four hours a day. Certainly your parents should have the right to make a decision as to whether or not they want to welcome and support another child in their own home. But they may have other reasons for objecting. If your parents remain unable to accept your decision about the pregnancy, all of you may benefit from some professional help.

CHAPTER FOUR

Overview of community resources

HOW TO SEEK INFORMATION

It would be convenient if you could call one central phone number and get whatever help and information you need regarding your pregnancy, but unfortunately it does not work that way. You need medical attention. You may also need adoption service, help in finding a place to stay, and financial assistance. When you call an agency, you may not even know what you need besides HELP!

You may find that you have to appeal to separate agencies for each thing. The procedure becomes frustrating and bewildering, as you bare your soul each time with no guarantee of results. Hopefully, somewhere along the way you will find someone who knows what is available in your particular locality. This person can help you to figure out what you do need and will advise you on how to proceed. But you will probably have to do the ground work on your own, and what follows will give you some idea of what to expect.

When you are pregnant and you are trying to be discreet about it, you can use the telephone to find out quite a bit without exposing yourself. A roll of dimes is a lot cheaper than bus or taxi fare all over town, not to mention taking time off from work or school, and the long and anxious moments in waiting rooms. Most doctors, lawyers, and social workers see patients or clients on an appointment basis which makes it a good idea to call ahead.

Approach the Yellow Pages of the phone book creatively. You can also call the local Medical Society or the Bar Association for names of doctors and lawyers, and for the names of clinics and the local Legal Aid Society. If you cannot find what you are looking for, call the Information operator. Do not be intimidated by her. Social agencies (including adoption services and maternity homes) are listed in the Yellow Pages under "Social Service and Welfare Organizations." Look through all of the listings, and call *any*body you think might be helpful. A brand new classification in the Yellow Pages of some phone books is "Problem Pregnancies."

When you make calls it is ideal if you have a number where people can call you back. It becomes complicated when you have to call from a pay phone during a coffee break or from a desk in the middle of a room with one hundred other people sitting around you. Remember that the person you are calling does not necessarily know why you are calling or where you are calling from, and he or she may not think to ask. Instead of breaking into a whisper, explain that you have a personal problem but at the moment you cannot talk freely. Hopefully, the person on the other end of the line will respond to this and offer you another time to call that will afford you more privacy.

Sometimes a friend or a relative can call for you, but since you are the one who is involved, many professional people will insist upon talking to you directly.

When you make a phone call, the way you present yourself and what you ask will make a great deal of difference in how you are received and what happens from there. If you are calling somebody you have already met or who is expecting your call, some form of rapport has already been established. But if you are calling a professional person or an agency for information, it is helpful to be aware of certain things.

Your call to most doctors, lawyers, and social workers will probably be answered by a secretary or a switchboard operator. In small offices the secretary knows what is going on, and she may be able to provide you with very general information over the phone. In larger offices the person who answers the phone may know only where to transfer your call. It is wise to make sure that you have the right person on the other end of the line before you start spilling out the story of your life. Secretaries can be very friendly and helpful, or they can seem preoccupied and distant. If you can win over a secretary, you may have acquired an ally who will be enormously helpful as you pursue whatever you need at this particular stage. If a secretary demands that you state your business, you can insist that the matter is confidential and that you would prefer to discuss it with the doctor or lawyer directly. In that case it is best to request an appointment and leave it at that.

You must remember that as long as you are using a telephone you remain an anonymous voice at the other end of the line. If the secretary sounds abrupt, it cannot have very much to do with you personally because she does not know you or anything about you. Most girls feel self-conscious and vulnerable about the fact that they are pregnant. Sometimes they expect to be rejected and treated roughly. If a secretary (or anyone else) sounds rude or hurried over the phone, it may be simply that she is in a hurry to go to lunch.

When you call for certain kinds of general information, the person at the other end of the line may ask you questions in order to be able to answer your questions, or in order to know to whom to refer your call. This is true for many social workers. The questions may seem personal or irrelevant, but specific facts may determine the answers to what you want to know. For example, you might be asked how old you are to determine whether or not you are a minor and will therefore require parental signatures. You may be asked where you live in case you are eligible for services in a particular section of the city. Or you may be asked the first day of your last menstrual period in order to establish how far along you are in the pregnancy. You may feel especially threatened if a secretary asks for your name. Perhaps she is asking only because she is required to fill out a routine form on each call as part of office procedures. If you feel it is unnecessary or inappropriate to give your name, say that you prefer not to leave your name. Considering the nature of your problem, most people will understand and accept that. If, however, you are pressured, make up a name.

Doctors and lawyers are usually reluctant to give information over the phone. In order to diagnose your particular problem, they may have to ask you a number of personal questions which can be awkward, offensive, and unfruitful when asked of a total stranger over the telephone. For this reason you will probably be encouraged to come into the office for an appointment. If you are worried about the cost, ask how much it will be at the time you make the appointment.

It is more difficult to generalize about contacting social workers because their jobs are much more varied, and so are their styles. Some of them will appear terribly matter-of-fact and practical, while you are about to explode inside. Others will focus on how you "feel" about the pregnancy, while all you care about is where you are going to stay tonight and whether she is going to issue you a rent order. Many social workers want to help you, but sometimes they have a peculiar way of going about it. (For more information about social workers, see pages 146–148.)

Another way of contacting people, of course, is by let-

ter. All doctors, lawyers, and social workers have a professional commitment to treat whatever information you offer
about yourself in confidence. If you are concerned about revealing your identity, make up a name and put it in care of
the name and address of a friend on a self-addressed envelope.
This may also be a good idea if you are trying to conceal
your pregnancy from your parents, a roommate, or whomever else you might be living with.

In writing to various organizations and agencies, you can
request that they reply using a plain envelope. Many organizations do this as a matter of policy out of respect for your
privacy in the community where you live. Otherwise, enclose
a stamped, self-addressed envelope to be sure no slip-ups
occur.

Some girls are a lot more concerned than others about
who finds out about the pregnancy. Blackmail is unusual in
this day and age, but every girl is entitled to privacy in con-
ducting her personal affairs.

SPECIFIC INDIVIDUALS AND AGENCIES

Some of the following individuals and social agencies might
be able to offer you guidance or help. Even if you have had a
baby before, you may find that services are different from
one state to another, or that they have expanded and im-
proved since your last experience. Many girls are reluctant to
contact the same agencies that have been helpful to them previously. They feel that perhaps they could be forgiven for
"making a mistake" the first time, but by now everyone expects them to know better. Some doctors or social workers
may be disappointed in you, but others will appreciate what it
must mean for you to go through the experience all over
again. Also they will be happy that you are able to return to
them when you need help.

Since agencies are called different names in different

counties and states, it is a good idea to scan the listings in the Yellow Pages of your phone book. If the agency you call does not have what you need, find out what it does have, and ask where else you might find what you are looking for.

Doctors

Doctors may be helpful in offering
    Morning-After Treatment
    Pregnancy testing
    Abortion referral
    Referral to a maternity home
    Adoption assistance
    Complete medical care, including follow-up

Some doctors are aloof or judgmental. You may have to try several before you find one who is sympathetic.

You may also want to consult someone about the emotional aspects of your situation. The chapter on counseling and therapy explains the difference between a psychiatrist, a psychoanalyst, a psychologist, and different kinds of social workers who are qualified to offer counseling.

Lawyers

Lawyers can be very helpful, especially if you have one as a personal friend. However, even if he is a personal friend or a relative, make sure that he has had at least some experience with the particular problem that is concerning you. There are many specialties within the field of law, and someone who works for a large business corporation or firm is not as likely to know about domestic matters (divorce, adoption, paternity) as a lawyer who has a general practice and who is active in community affairs. Lawyers can advise you regarding

    Filing a paternity suit against the baby's father
    Adoption procedures

Your rights in applying for financial assistance from the
State Department of Welfare

You may have to shop around until you find one you like and
trust. If your lawyer will be drafting adoption papers for you
make sure this is not his first experience. This point will be
discussed in more detail in the chapter on adoption.

Planned Parenthood
Some Planned Parenthood agencies are more progressive than
others in the services they offer. Policies are somewhat controlled by the laws of the counties and states in which the
agencies operate. Planned Parenthood helps families and individuals to have only those babies they consciously want and
plan for. They may be able to help you with

> Morning-After pills
> Pregnancy test
> Pregnancy counseling and referral
> Abortion information
> Referral to medical care
> Contraceptive advice and information
> Premarital or marriage counseling
> Venereal disease information, testing, and treatment

Some agencies require you to be eighteen or over in order to
receive service without the consent of your parents; even so,
you are not always asked to show proof of your age. A complete list of Planned Parenthood agencies may be found in
the Appendix.

Child Welfare Department
This organization, a department within the State Department
of Social Welfare, is a good place to call for information
about
> Adoption service and counseling

Some Child Welfare Departments will also offer
  Financial assistance
  Medicaid—financial assistance to cover the cost of your
    medical expenses
  Help in finding living arrangements

Maternity Homes

All maternity homes offer
  Residential care for the "unwed mother" during the
    last weeks or months of her pregnancy
  Medical care, including arrangements for hospitaliza-
    tion and delivery

A few homes also offer adoption service, but most of them
rely on other agencies in the community to handle child
placement. For more information see the chapter on maternity homes.

Adoption Agencies

These agencies go by a variety of names, some of which
sound very old-fashioned. Many adoption agencies which are
sponsored by religious groups limit service to members of one
specific faith; others are more flexible. It may be best to call
several agencies to find out which one offers the most satisfac-
tory service. For more information see the chapter on adoption.

Family Service Agencies

Large communities often have several family service agencies.
Among the more familiar ones are Jewish Family Service, Lutheran Family Service, and Catholic Social Service. Some of
these agencies limit their services to members of their own

faiths, while others are more flexible. Family service agencies which are staffed by social workers may be able to help with

Referral to maternity services in the community
Financial assistance
Counseling

Abortion Referral

More and more people are involved in helping women to get abortions. Some are conscientious and humane individuals who are dedicated to the cause of women's rights and legalizing abortion. Others are involved for profit, but may still offer reliable information. Here are some numbers to try:

Local Clergy Consultation Service on Abortion (possibly listed under "Problem Pregnancies")
Planned Parenthood
Suicide Prevention
"Switchboard" or "Hot Line"
Local hospital
Friends
College medical center
Free clinic

Also check in underground newspapers. For more information on abortions see Chapter Six.

Community Chest–United Crusade Sponsored Information and Referral Services

United Good Neighbor
United Community Service Bureau

These referral services have been developed to varying degrees in different cities in the United States. You may or may not be able to find a knowledgeable person to help you. Because this organization is sponsored by community funds it is not a likely source for abortion referrals, but you may be able to find out about other services.

Suicide Prevention Centers and Local Switchboards

These centers function in a variety of ways. Some employ volunteers who answer calls directly. Others depend on a switchboard operator who directs the calls to a psychiatrist. Either way, you should be able to find someone with a sympathetic manner and maybe some ideas on where you can go for various kinds of help.

Maternity and Infant Care Projects

A list of these programs is included in the Appendix at the back of this book. This project is sponsored by the United States Children's Bureau and is administered by local health departments. Eligibility includes women who are pregnant and who

> Live in a particular district
> Have low incomes
> Have medical or social problems which may complicate
> the pregnancy, for example:
>> High blood pressure
>> Toxemia
>> Rh factor
>> Single girls
>> Younger girls, especially those under 16

These projects offer

> Complete medical care, which includes
>> Prenatal
>> Delivery
>> Postpartum
>> Infant medical supervision
> Teen-age clinic and school classes

Individual and group work
Dental care
Homemaking assistance
Baby-sitting
Transportation
Nutrition consultation
Health education
Casework consultation and referral

This is an excellent and comprehensive service for the women and girls to whom it is available.

YWCA

The YWCA may offer

A program for pregnant teen-agers
Single mothers' groups
Education for childbirth classes

You can call and find out if they have such programs or if they know of any elsewhere in the city.

The Red Cross

The Red Cross limits most of its services to legal dependents of servicemen. However, if your boyfriend is in the service and you want to locate him, they will be helpful. The Red Cross also offers classes in education for childbirth and baby care to anyone who is interested.

Youth Emergency Services

More and more of these free clinics are becoming available to young people who need help. Many of them are primarily concerned with drug problems, but they may also be good referral sources for questions related to pregnancy.

International Service Agencies

These agencies have been established to help immigrants and individuals who are not American citizens. The social workers can often speak several languages, and are familiar with some of the international codes that relate to citizenship, paternity, and rights of non-citizens. If you are involved in an international problem this is a good agency to contact. Look carefully in the Yellow Pages under "Social Service and Welfare Organizations" for what might be an international institute or agency.

Traveler's Aid

If you are in a strange city and do not know what to do, contact Traveler's Aid for immediate advice on whom to call for further help.

Ministers, Priests, Rabbis

You may find that a religious advisor can be very helpful. Some have old-fashioned attitudes and may take an arbitrary stand on what you should do about keeping or relinquishing your baby for adoption. However, some religious leaders are progressive and enlightened in their thinking, and may be able to help you in a variety of ways. Perhaps you know or have heard of someone whom you could consult for support and guidance.

School and College Personnel— Local Unified School District

Any of the following may be helpful:

Teachers and professors
School counselors
Principals and deans
School nurses

It is impossible to generalize about what to expect from school personnel. In some schools a pregnancy warrants immediate expulsion. In other schools it is such a common event that there is a routine procedure on what the young woman is to do. You probably know what the attitude is at your particular school and can anticipate whether or not you will be treated kindly. Many high schools require that you drop out and return to a different school after your baby is born. Sometimes a home teacher is provided so that you can keep up with your studies during your pregnancy. In some school districts, projects are being set up especially for pregnant teenagers.

If you are not sure what to do, call the local school district office and ask how they treat pregnant girls. (For more information see the chapter on school programs.)

On the college level it is also difficult to make generalizations, but usually you can sense whether the administration will take a kindly attitude towards your problem. If you suspect that the college will be uncooperative, contact some of the outside sources mentioned in the earlier part of this chapter before you reveal your situation to campus authorities.

CHAPTER FIVE

Marriage

It is difficult to know in what sequence to place a chapter on marriage, because marriage itself will not alter the fact that you are pregnant. It simply spares you the disgrace of becoming an *unmarried* mother.

Sometimes marriage is utterly out of the question, for example, when the baby's father is already married to someone else whom he is not planning to divorce in order to marry you. Or maybe by the time you find out you are pregnant you cannot stand the father or he cannot stand you. Sometimes the girl has to become pregnant in order for a couple to realize that they really do not want to get married after all. In other situations the pregnancy implies too much responsibility, and it frightens away an otherwise devoted fiancé.

Sometimes one of the families is strongly opposed to the idea of marriage and it becomes too much for the young couple to handle on their own. Another realistic consideration is whether or not the couple can afford to marry and support a baby without interrupting long-range educational or vocational commitments.

Some couples are able to admit frankly to themselves and to each other that they do not feel ready to take on the responsibilities of marriage and a family. They may want to consider it later on, but they do not want to be forced into marriage by circumstances they had not anticipated. It becomes complicated and unhappy when one person feels ready and the other one does not.

Of course you cannot get married if you do not know who the father is or where he is.

Marriage itself means different things to different people, and under these particular circumstances, it is difficult to advocate a position that is especially for it or against it. Statistics show that the divorce rate is considerably higher for couples who marry specifically to legitimize a pregnancy.

If you love each other and you were planning to get married eventually anyway, and you are both somewhat enthusiastic about the baby, although you had not planned to have him quite so soon, you should by all means go ahead and get married. But if your feelings toward each other are less than that, you should consider several possibilities before you decide to marry. For one thing, make sure you are definitely pregnant!

If you get married you are more or less committing yourself to keep the baby. This is fine, of course, if you are sure you *want* a baby right now. But if you are at all unsure, you must realize that once you are married it is terribly awkward for you to give your first child up for adoption. The pregnancy may be socially embarrassing for you and your family for the next six or seven months, but the responsibility involved in rearing a child lasts for years! This is something to think about. Parents who are overly eager for their daughters to marry should think about this too.

You might decide to get married because you believe that your child deserves to have two parents instead of one. But many children actually grow up with only one parent, even though their parents may be legally married. Marriage is not a guarantee that two people will love each other and live together as a stable family unit.

Girls sometimes rush into marriage and promptly miscarry. Then what do you do with the unwanted husband?

Marriage legitimizes the pregnancy so that you do not have to go into hiding, but it may also cause unnecessary legal problems. One family insisted upon marriage as soon as they found that their daughter was pregnant. Her "husband" went into the service, and she checked into a maternity home. The two never saw each other again. Her family kept the marriage *and* the pregnancy a secret, which made the marriage completely unnecessary. From the beginning the girl was sure she wanted to give up the baby for adoption. Many months later when it was time to sign the relinquishment papers, her husband had to be located for his signature. The family then had to go to the expense of hiring a lawyer to file for an annulment. In the last analysis, the marriage accomplished nothing except additional complications and expenses.

Another girl who planned to keep her baby was reluctant to tell the real father that she was going to have his child. Instead, a dear friend agreed to marry her so that the baby would have a legal father. He and the girl never made any pretense about living together as man and wife. Also, she promised she would never make demands on his income. When this girl's savings ran out and she needed financial assistance, she was ineligible because of her "husband's" legal responsibility to support her and the child. The whole situation became awkward and complicated, and in the long run the marriage caused many more problems than it solved.

If you find yourself marrying *only* in order to give the baby a "name," you and your husband-to-be would be wise to consult a lawyer who is familiar with domestic affairs so that you both know what you are getting into. I suggest you consult a lawyer *before* you get married. For one thing, the fellow will be assuming the legal responsibility to pay child-support for the next twenty-one years whether you become divorced later on or not. An attorney may be able to suggest less complicated ways of having the birth certificate appear that your baby was legitimate.

Maybe now that you are pregnant, you are convinced that marriage and a baby are exactly what you want. However, if they are not exactly what you had in mind at this time, you might want to consider some of the alternatives which follow.

CHAPTER SIX

Abortion

One way to avoid becoming an "unmarried mother" is to get married. The other way is to avoid becoming a mother, by getting an abortion. Abortion is a difficult subject for most of us. The word alone triggers off a variety of attitudes and emotions. Since decisions regarding an abortion are controlled by state laws and court decisions, women are sometimes forced to turn to illegal means.

However, attitudes seem to be changing quickly, and many states may soon revise or at least review their existing laws. New York, for example, recently revised its 140-year old abortion law, allowing abortions to be performed during the first twenty-four weeks of pregnancy. The decision is entirely up to each woman and her doctor. Under this law you are not required to be a resident of the state of New York in order to be eligible for an abortion. Several states have liberalized laws, but require that you be a resident of that particular state. The laws also vary in establishing the point in pregnancy after which a legal abortion may not be performed. Since these laws vary considerably from state to state you should check with your doctor, Planned Parenthood, or an abortion referral service to see what the law is in your particular state. As abortion laws become more relaxed, the next problem will be finding enough doctors who are willing to perform abortions at the rate they are requested at a price everyone is able to pay.

Some girls, the instant they find out they are pregnant, consider no other alternative than to get an abortion as soon as possible. Others, no matter how upset they are about being pregnant, would not consider an abortion. Still others would get an abortion if they knew where to get one safely, or if they could afford it. Some girls never give it much serious thought, one way or another.

KINDS OF ABORTION

What is an abortion? According to Lawrence Lader, "Abortion, in medical terms, is the induced termination of pregnancy before the normal fetus has attained viability, or the capacity for life outside the womb. The word applies only to intentional termination as opposed to spontaneous abortion, which occurs when fetal growth is impaired and is frequently referred to as *miscarriage.*"

Abortions are performed in several ways, depending upon how advanced the pregnancy is and who is doing it under what conditions. Up until the first twelve weeks, counting from the first day of the last normal menstrual period, either a D and C (dilation and curettage) or the vacuum pump method are recommended.

For a standard D and C, the patient is admitted to a hospital or clinic preferably the night before the operation is scheduled. During surgery anesthesia is used to reduce the pain. With a special instrument the doctor goes up through the vaginal opening and stretches the mouth of the cervix so that he can gently scrape out the inside of the uterus. Medication is used to help the uterus contract back to its normal size and to control bleeding. Altogether the patient may remain in the hospital for one or two days.

The vacuum pump method, which has been widely used

in the Soviet Union, has recently been introduced in hospitals and clinics all over the United States. Generally it is found to be quicker and safer than a D and C. Blood loss is reduced; risk of infection and other complications is less, and it can be performed in a doctor's office instead of requiring an overnight stay in the hospital. (Even so you are advised to take it easy for several days afterwards.)

After twelve weeks the methods for abortion become more complicated. One method, called a hysterotomy, involves making a small incision into the uterus through the abdomen. This leaves a small scar. A method which has been developed more recently involves the replacement of the amniotic fluid with a salt solution. This is done under local anesthetic by carefully inserting a needle into the uterus through the abdomen. The saline solution induces labor within a number of hours, and the products of conception are eventually expelled through the vagina. This method may involve several days in the hospital. It can be extremely dangerous unless it is performed by skilled experts in the best of hospital conditions.

When your body, for its own reasons, terminates the pregnancy it ejects what in medical terms is called a "blighted (or imperfect) ovum." Spontaneous abortions most often occur by the twelfth week of pregnancy. Early signs of a spontaneous abortion are backache, abdominal cramps, and often a bloody discharge. If the pregnancy ends in this fashion, it is a good idea to see a doctor to make sure that you are all right. If all of the contents are not expelled from the uterus they may cause infection.

Self-Induced Abortion

Another kind of abortion is a self-induced abortion. Women have employed a variety of methods for aborting themselves since the beginning of time. These include everything from jumping off the kitchen table to inserting a variety of sharp objects up through the vagina. Abortion is basically a simple surgical process when it is performed by a specialist in a hospital; but it is a dangerous business when women try it themselves. No marketable drugs that can be taken orally or by injection (including quinine and ergot preparations) will reliably produce an abortion. Some women drink down frightening mixtures of household cleansers with the hopes of aborting, but anything strong enough to destroy the fetus will very likely destroy you as well. The same principle applies for solutions that women inject into their vaginas.

One reason self-induced abortion is so dangerous is that during pregnancy the uterus becomes soft and enlarged. The risk is that you may perforate the wall of the uterus. Excessive bleeding and hemorrhaging result, and if the bleeding is not stopped quickly, you may die. Another hazard, of course, is infection. If you want an abortion, many sources of professional help are available today which include social workers, doctors, clergy, and the staff at the various agencies listed in the Appendix of this book; any attempt to abort yourself is foolish and dangerous.

SUGGESTIONS FOR PROCEEDING

As soon as you suspect that you are pregnant, it is essential to confirm the diagnosis before you go any further. (Refer to Chapter Two for information regarding pregnancy tests.) Some women become so panicky that they submit to an abortion when they are not even pregnant. When the operation is performed legally by a licensed physician, he requires diagnostic proof of the fact that you are pregnant. However, many of the abortionists who have to operate under cover have neither the time nor the motivation to determine if you are pregnant, and they operate regardless. So before you do *anything* find out if you are pregnant.

If you are pregnant and you are sure that you want an abortion, it is wise to act immediately. The earlier in the pregnancy you have the operation, the less complicated it is, and it usually costs less. If you are not sure if you want an abortion, whatever you do, do not let someone else—your boyfriend or your parents or your friends—put so much pressure on you that you find yourself in surgery before you have had a chance to think this out on your own. Abortion may seem like the quickest and most practical solution to everybody else, but considering what *you* may have to go through to get one, making the decision can be quite traumatic. Perhaps you can consult a professional person to find out what is involved. Abortion is not the best answer for everyone. You have a right to think through whether or not this is what *you* want.

In most states in the United States legal abortion must be prescribed and approved by a committee of doctors on the grounds that it will save the life of the mother. Other reasons such as rape, incest, or the likelihood of producing a deformed child are usually not sufficient grounds for requesting a legal (therapeutic) abortion. Few hospital boards would approve an abortion on the simple grounds that a girl is not married. Unless you are lucky enough to find a sympathetic and discreet doctor who will either abort you himself or refer you to a colleague for that purpose, you may have to resort to a more underground approach.

In several states a therapeutic abortion can be obtained in order to preserve the *mental* as well as the physical health of the mother. Some doctors are very strict in their interpretations of "mental" health; others feel that any woman who wants an abortion should have one, and it would be detrimental to her mental health to deny her one. Even many women who live in these states do not realize that they can get legal, therapeutic abortions in reputable hospitals as long as they have letters from two psychiatrists recommending the operation.

In the meantime, more and more groups and organizations are springing up that offer abortion counseling. You will find some of them mentioned on page 38 in Chapter Four. Local organizations are listed in the Appendix at the back of this book.

If you call one of the Clergy Consultation Services you will hear a recording which gives you the names and phone numbers of several volunteer clergymen. You are then to call one of them and make an appointment for a personal interview. In order to spare themselves and you from "false alarms," they request that you bring a confirmation of pregnancy to the appointment. Some people expect that the clergymen will have the facilities for performing the abortion right there in his office, but his role as a counselor is to discuss with you what you want to do about your pregnancy. If you both feel that an abortion is indicated he may be able to arrange for you to get one. If you decide that you do not want an abortion, he can help you to make other arrangements.

Many women who are unable to obtain abortions within the United States travel to other countries such as Japan, where the operation is legal. The cost of an abortion in Japan seems to vary widely; in some cases it depends upon how advanced the pregnancy is. Round-trip fare alone from San Francisco to Tokyo costs between $680 and $722, depending on the time of year you go. At the moment England is also a popular place to go for legal abortions, but many of the doctors object to the large number of requests that take them away from their regular practices. Consequently, the policy there may change at any time.

Some countries have relaxed policies on abortion in serving their own citizens but this same leniency does not always apply to foreign visitors. For many years, Sweden has been thought of as a country that readily performs abortions; but in fact, until very recently many Swedes have been denied abortions, and have had to go abroad to England or Poland to have the operation. Before you spend your last nickel and hop on a plane, make sure you have accurate knowledge about the place you are going and what to expect when you get there.

In pregnancy counseling or counseling on abortion, each girl or woman should be given a chance to express her anxieties about having an abortion, especially if it is to be performed illegally. Some counselors are so sold on abortion for everyone that they fail to realize that some women may have mixed feelings. In some counseling interviews there is so much practical information to cover that there is no opportunity to consider the quivers a girl may be feeling in the pit of her stomach. If you find you are scared, say so, and hopefully the counselor will slow down enough to let you take a deep breath before he continues with his instructions.

COST OF ABORTIONS

Some people do not realize that abortions cost money. It does not matter whether you have an abortion in the United States or elsewhere. If the abortion is performed illegally, of course it will not be covered by your medical insurance plan. In order to obtain an illegal abortion you must almost always be prepared to pay at least several hundred dollars. Occasionally you can get an illegal abortion for less than $200, but abortionists feel entitled to charge as much as they like because of the risks they are taking by breaking the law.

Several hundred dollars in cash for an abortion may seem like a lot of money. It is! But it costs at least that to go into a hospital and deliver a baby. Unfortunately, once you are pregnant, unless you abort spontaneously, it will probably cost you (or somebody) a pretty penny, whether you have an abortion or continue the pregnancy.

Sometimes *therapeutic* abortions are covered by medical insurance plans. In some states the Medicaid program in the Welfare department will pay for a *legal* abortion. If you are eligible for a legal abortion in your state, you should inquire as soon as possible at the Welfare department or at the hospital where you plan to have your operation to see if Medicaid will cover the expense.

ILLEGAL ABORTIONS

Whether an abortion is legal or illegal will depend upon the laws in your particular state. Remember, though, that just because the abortion is illegal is no reason why it should be performed under conditions which are unsafe. No matter how anxious and frightened you are, ask the doctor or abortionist what method he plans to use. Methods such as the insertion of a catheter tube into the vagina or the pumping of any solution, including air, Lysol, and soap compounds, into the uterus are extremely dangerous and may cause death, sterility, or a variety of serious infections.

Sometimes even though your doctor cannot in any way participate in the abortion himself, if he knows you are about to have one elsewhere he may give you antibiotics to reduce the likelihood of infection. If this is the case, he will probably encourage you to come back afterwards to make sure that the operation was complete and successful and that no infection has developed.

Most illegal abortionists do not do their own follow-up care. In order to minimize the chances of being arrested, they want you out of their office as soon after the operation as possible. Sometimes this means that the abortion is not complete by the time you get back to your hotel or apartment, in which case you may need additional medical care. Following an abortion, regardless of the circumstances, you should be checked by a responsible physician. If you are reluctant to go to your private doctor, call the Clergy Consultation Service or a Planned Parenthood office for a referral to someone who will be sympathetic to your situation. If you begin to hemorrhage, or if you develop a fever or other signs of infection, do not be foolhardy. Get yourself to a doctor or a hospital without delay!

You are more likely to encounter harassment from doctors and police officers in a county hospital than you would in a small, private hospital. However, you are not obliged to give out any information about the abortion. You have civil rights like any other citizen, and you cannot be forced to give incriminating evidence against yourself or against the doctor who performed the operation. If you are surrounded by hostile doctors and police, demand legal counsel. Harassment of this kind happens occasionally, but let us hope that it does not happen to you.

AFTER THE ABORTION

Assuming that your abortion goes well and there are no complications whatever, it is still important to take things easy until your body has had a chance to return to normal. Remember that your body has been gradually undergoing various changes, and it will need time to recover. Also the operation has left your uterus open and vulnerable. Until it has a chance to return to its normal size, which takes about a month, you are advised not to put *any*thing into your vagina. "Anything" includes douches, Tampax, and penises.

When you consult your doctor about having an abortion, or when you go in for follow-up care, ask him about birth control. The loop can be inserted by a doctor as soon as the abortion is complete. Birth control pills may be started between four to six weeks after an abortion, or you can go in and have a diaphragm fitted sometime after six weeks.

What about psychological repercussions from having an abortion? You may have fantasies from time to time about the child you never had. But many women who have never been pregnant have fantasies about children they never had. Most women who have mixed feelings about abortion manage to avoid having the operation, perhaps by waiting until it is too late. However, if you find you are having trouble overcoming the whole experience, it is a good idea to seek psychiatric counseling. Refer to the chapter on counseling and therapy for information about this kind of help.

CHAPTER SEVEN

The problem gets bigger...

For the remainder of this book we shall assume that you are definitely pregnant and that you are going to continue the pregnancy. The next big question is whether or not you are going to try and conceal the pregnancy, and if so, from whom. Of course it would be easier if you could stay right where you are and go about your business as any properly married pregnant woman would do. You may have no idea, however, how the people around you will react to the fact that you are single and pregnant, and it may be better to leave than to stay and find out. Sometimes you *do* know how they will react and, being sensitive to sarcastic and unkind remarks, you find yourself packing your suitcases. Sometimes everybody knows and is reasonably nice about the whole thing, but you decide to leave anyway for a change of scenery.

If you are over twenty-one, technically you are free to stay or go as you please. If you have piles of money (at least $1,700), you can go almost anywhere in the United States (allowing $200 for transportation), and you will probably be able to live modestly for about four months (4 × $200 = $800) and pay your medical expenses ($600-$700). Sometimes inexpensive living arrangements can be worked out. Sometimes financial aid is available from the Welfare Department. Sometimes, but not often, a girl in the latter part of her pregnancy can find employment so that she can continue to support herself. However, unless you have a substantial amount of cash it is unwise to leave the state where you have legal residence. In your own state you will always be given priority in regard to services (assuming your state has services!). This applies to maternity homes, adoption service, medical care, and financial assistance. In some states, if you are a nonresident the most help you will get, if any, will be a one-way ticket back home, which may be the last place in the world you want to go.

If you are between 18 and 21, your freedom to stay or go elsewhere, especially without parental knowledge and consent, will depend upon the laws defining the rights of minors both in your own state and in the state to which you travel. You will need a substantial amount of cash. Before you go anywhere, call the local Legal Aid Society, the Child Welfare Department, or a local maternity home to find out what the laws are in your area. Especially important is having access to medical care without the signed consent from at least one of your parents or your guardian. If you are considering giving your baby up for adoption, also ask if you will be allowed to sign the final adoption papers without the signatures of your parents or your guardian. Every state has different requirements, and you should know what problems may lie ahead of you.

If you are under 18, even if you are very rich and adventurous, you are probably going to run into difficulty if you wander very far away from home without telling *some*one. Even though having a baby is a natural and spontaneous phenomenon, you will need help along the way. Because of your age, in most states a doctor is not allowed to touch you without permission from a parent or guardian. Anyone who offers you shelter (friends, relatives, maternity homes, boarding houses) can be charged with kidnaping, which is a risk many people will not take, no matter how much they want to help you. If you are under 18, and you are reluctant to tell your parents that you are pregnant, review Chapters Three and Four and see if you cannot find at least *one* suggestion that will help you decide what to do next.

Whether you stay in your own community or embark on an extended "vacation" elsewhere, there are basic services you will need during the remaining months of your pregnancy, regardless of your age. The chapters that follow will give you some idea of what these services are, how to apply for them, and generally what to expect. The picture has to remain a very general one because communities are so different in the types of services they offer and the spirit in which they offer them.

Some of the services you require will relate directly to the pregnancy, and there will be no question in anybody's mind about what your situation is. However, unless you appear unusually young, most people will assume you are married, especially if you wear a wedding band. This applies to people on buses and in department stores, and even many staff members at the clinic or hospital where you go for medical care.

Every woman feels self-conscious when she is pregnant. It is an awkward sensation to have your abdomen swell out beyond your nose and your toes. Think how self-conscious you feel about much more minor changes in your appearance, a different hair-style or a pimple on your chin. If you sense that people are staring at you, it is not because they suspect you are not married. People stare at anything out of the ordinary, and it may be your tummy and nothing more that attracts attention. So keep your head high and a twinkle in your eye instead of betraying what you may be feeling inside by rounding your shoulders and avoiding people's eyes.

It becomes a little more awkward when you find your-self becoming friendly with the clerk at the grocery store or going back to the same hairdresser to have your hair done. Questions about your husband and the expected baby are intended as friendly overtures, but you find yourself on the spot because these people are kind and you do not want to lie to them. And yet you do not want to tell them the truth either. Someone may even surprise you with a baby shower. After the baby is born, the situation becomes even more difficult, especially if you have given him up for adop-tion. Now what are you supposed to say?

Another problem arises when unsuspecting friends or relatives arrive in town and look you up. They cannot under-stand how you can possibly be *so* busy that you do not have a single moment to get together with them. Sometimes family crises occur and there is no acceptable explanation for why you are not available to come home in the emer-gency.

If only you could be open and honest it would be so much easier. Instead you are perhaps to discover that you can become a much better liar than you ever suspected.

CHAPTER EIGHT

Planning through a maternity home

People are very curious about maternity homes, especially if they have never been inside one. Perhaps what follows will give you an idea of what they are like.

WHAT THEY ARE

The 1966 directory of *Maternity Homes and Residential Facilities for Unmarried Mothers* lists 194 homes in the United States. Almost every state has at least one home, including three in Washington, D.C. The states which do not have homes listed are New Hampshire, South Carolina, Mississippi, Utah, Wyoming, and Nevada. Possibly some of these states have established homes since 1966.

People go to maternity homes for several different reasons, but most commonly we think of a maternity home as a place to go and hide. In many maternity homes the girls use only their first names so that they remain anonymous even to each other. Only members of the staff know the real identities of the girls. Also the homes have unlisted phone numbers for the residents so that suspicious friends and relatives cannot call and check up on Susie, who mysteriously disappeared last week. Addresses are often listed in care of post office boxes or they are masked in some other way so that girls cannot be readily traced to a well-known maternity home in the community. Many maternity homes have a mail courtesy service. For example, let's say you enter one of the three homes in Philadelphia. In the meantime, you want your friends to think you are vacationing in Denver. An arrangement can be made to route all your mail through one of the homes in Denver so that it will be properly post-marked. Of course it is a different matter if someone tries to *visit* you in Denver!

Often when a girl enters a home she is immediately struck by all of the gimmicks that are used to disguise or conceal her identity. Sometimes these gimmicks are so much a part of the orientation that everyone loses sight of the fact that girls enter maternity homes for other reasons than to hide. Sometimes a girl has been forced to leave her own home and has no other place to go. Or perhaps she goes to a maternity home to be with other girls in the same situation.

Sometimes girls go to maternity homes because they do not know how to coordinate the various services they need. A maternity home offers a girl a place to stay and makes sure that she has medical care, adoption service, counseling, and financial aid if she is eligible to receive it. A few of the homes have programs so that school-age girls can keep up with their studies.

Regardless of the general atmosphere and attitude of the home toward "unmarried mothers," the girls themselves offer some degree of emotional support to one another. When a girl enters a home, at least she does not have to explain or apologize to the others for her condition. Whatever concerns or fears she may have about the pregnancy and childbirth she can share with others instead of being left to muse and fantasize by herself. Some girls gain from the experience of living with other girls in a group.

Many of the existing homes were started many years ago

as emergency shelters for single, pregnant girls who would only bring shame to their families if they stayed at home. These shelters, which offered solace and comfort to "poor, wayward girls" were usually sponsored by religious groups. The people at the shelters, although they did not condone the girls' behavior, appreciated their need and offered protection and care through their period of confinement. Most of the homes today (about 85 percent) are still supported and run by religious groups which express much the same attitude toward single, pregnant women that was characteristic at the beginning of this century. This is one of the reasons the common stereotype of the maternity home remains so bleak.

Upon entering a home a girl often expects to be treated as a criminal of some kind. Too often condescending attitudes of staff members, along with many restrictions and regulations, reinforce her impression that she has done something "wrong." For example, it make a tremendous difference if housekeeping tasks are assigned as part of a cooperative effort to keep things clean and comfortable or if they are assigned as punishment. It also makes a difference if a girl is asked to be in at eight o'clock for her own protection because the home is located in a rough section of the city, or if she has to be in at eight o'clock every evening as a penalty for being pregnant. Everyone becomes rebellious and resentful when rules are treated with more respect than the people who are obliged to follow them.

Most of the homes in the United States (about 70 percent) are run by either local Catholic organizations, the Salvation Army, or the Florence Crittenton Association. The remaining 30 percent of the homes are run by diverse religious groups: one Quaker, one Jewish, one Episcopal, five Lutheran, two Baptist, five Methodist, and so forth. A few are run as social agencies within a community and probably have less of a religious bias. Many of the Florence Crittenton homes were originated by religious groups, and continue to include religion as an important part of their programs.

Church attendance is compulsory for over one-third of the girls who enter maternity homes in the United States, and it is strongly encouraged for many more. In other words, many pregnant girls are required to attend church services as part of their maternity care. Naturally this creates a punitive atmosphere, instead of a constructive environment which deals realistically with questions about family planning and sex education.

Maternity homes, which are licensed residences for pregnant women, can be quite large or rather small. Sometimes family homes have been converted to accommodate up to ten girls at a time. Most of the homes are large enough to house between twenty and forty girls. These include beautiful old mansions which have been remodeled. Newer homes have been constructed as dormitories, and tend to have a more clinical atmosphere.

A variety of people make up the staff at a maternity home. Catholic homes are staffed by nuns, and Salvation Army homes are staffed by Brigadiers, Captains, and other officials of the Army. Many of these women have had at least some training in social work. Florence Crittenton homes are directed and staffed by social workers. The social work staff is usually small compared to the nursing staff, which must be available to the girls on a twenty-four-hour basis. (Overall medical care will be discussed further on.) Some maternity homes also employ consulting psychiatrists or psychologists to work with girls who have outstanding problems. The staff at most homes usually includes a housemother, a housekeeper, a cook, a group-worker to organize recreational activities, and office workers. Sometimes volunteers from the outside community donate services and time. Other members of the staff may include a chaplain, a librarian, a language teacher, and a public health nurse to teach classes in childbirth.

Many maternity homes are located in the run-down sections of town. This is usually because the home was established many years ago when this may have still been a fashionable section of the city. For many homes the cost of relocating remains prohibitive. Other homes, of course, are more attractively located.

WHAT THEY OFFER

Some homes include a clinic and a delivery room on the premises. Doctors make regular visits and are called in when a girl goes into labor. Other homes are located in the wings of large hospitals. This is generally true of the Salvation Army homes. Many homes that previously provided their own delivery rooms and nurseries are beginning to affiliate with hospitals in the community. Generally it is felt that a large hospital has the staff and facilities to handle any emergency that may occur during delivery. A maternity home, operating on a much smaller scale, cannot afford to maintain teams of specialists as well as expensive and complicated equipment.

A few of the homes which handle adoption have nursery facilities to accommodate the babies while the girl and the adopting family are completing adoption procedures. Sometimes the home makes all of the adoption arrangements but the child is housed in a separate nursery or foster home. Most of the time the entire adoption process is handled through an entirely different agency. This will be discussed in more detail in the chapter on adoption.

The primary function of most maternity homes is to provide a certain number of girls with shelter and food during the last months or weeks of pregnancy. In recent years some homes have extended their services to include outpatient arrangements of various kinds.

Some homes, for example, place younger girls in foster families within the community. This may be the best arrangement for girls with special problems or when bed space is filled within the home. Foster-home care may also be the best plan when a young girl must be away from her own family for a long period of time. In some states foster care is cheaper than residential maternity care. Sometimes a girl stays in foster care during most of her pregnancy, but is admitted into the home a few weeks before she is due to deliver. In any case, the homes try to keep an eye on the foster families. In the meantime the girls use the medical and counseling facilities of the home on an outpatient basis.

Many homes also affiliate with a certain number of "mutual service" or "wage" homes. Since maternity care is costly, many girls prefer to stay with families where they can babysit and do light housework in exchange for room and board. Sometimes the arrangement includes a small salary. Some girls stay in a mutual service home throughout the pregnancy, whereas others may enter the home shortly before delivery. Whether or not the girl actually enters the home as a resident, most of the services, such as medical care, adoption, and counseling, are available to her as an outpatient. Some of the advantages and disadvantages of mutual service homes will be discussed in the chapter on other living arrangements.

Several homes have opened special centers for school-age girls who continue living in their own homes but who come to the center to participate in classes and group discussions during the day. They may also come for different kinds of activities and for clinic care. Such programs are most commonly located in ghetto areas where the emphasis is on service rather than on concealing the pregnancy.

Most homes require that a girl remain in residence for at least ten days after delivery. For some girls this becomes pure torture. Separation from the baby is painful enough without dragging it out. Others are eager to go home or to return to school or work by a certain deadline. On the other hand, for other girls, ten days may seem hardly long enough to recover from delivery, to make a final decision about the baby, and to figure out where to go next. Several homes have established halfway houses or apartments where girls can stay after delivery while they look for jobs and begin to re-establish themselves in the community.

Once the idea of adoption became popular, almost every girl who stayed at a maternity home gave up her baby. However, nowadays more and more girls are deciding to keep their babies. Some maternity homes have initiated services to single mothers who keep their babies, and a few have established apartments where girls can stay with their babies until they feel they can manage on their own. Most maternity homes, however, are concerned exclusively with the pregnancy. They feel that after-care services should be the responsibility of other agencies in the community.

You now have a very *general* idea of what a maternity home is. A maternity home may provide a profound, meaningful experience to one girl, and be a living nightmare to another. It depends on the home, and it depends on the girl. Remember that other alternatives besides maternity homes may be available, and it might be a good idea to consider several different plans before you make a final decision about where to go and what to do.

WHEN AND HOW TO APPLY
When and how do you apply to a maternity home? You should apply as early as you can since most maternity homes

have long waiting lists of applicants. Even if you do not plan to enter a home for another three or four months, you should write or call and make sure your name is on the list so that a space will be reserved when it is time for you to be admitted. This is terribly important.

Most people initiate contact with a maternity home by calling or writing for information. You in turn will probably be asked for whatever information is required to determine whether or not you are eligible for admission to that particular home. If you are applying by letter, it is suggested that you include the following information about yourself:

Your age

The first day of your last menstrual period

Whether or not you have had the pregnancy confirmed by a doctor

Your general state of health

What you are doing now: whether you are working or in school

The general state of your finances: how you intend to pay for room and board, medical care, and other expenses, such as travel

Whether or not your family knows about the pregnancy

Whether you have already made a definite decision to keep or give up the baby, or if you are still undecided

The state and county in which you are a legal resident

Your letter will probably be filled with at least as many questions. The above information will make it easier for the home to give you the appropriate answers. Some homes will ask about your racial background and the racial background of the baby's father. Often this is to anticipate problems in placing the baby with an adoptive family. Most homes still cater essentially to "nice," white, middle-class girls, but most of them, at least on paper, no longer deny admission to girls simply because they are members of a minority group.

Relatively few black girls are found in most maternity homes. This is *partly* because the black community is not aware of the fact that such a service is available. Also black mothers do not ordinarily consider sending their daughters away to a strange (white) place at a time when they need to be loved and cared for at home. Many girls assume that a maternity home is a place where you go and give up your baby (in many cases it is). In the black community families do not give up their own flesh and blood (partly because the choice has never been available to them), and they have evolved a tradition of looking after their own as well as they can. Finally, many black girls are turned away simply because they wait until too late in the pregnancy to apply, and space is not available.

Many homes have formal restrictions of one kind or another. Some of the reasons you may be denied admission are:

Marital Status. About one-fourth of the homes will not admit you unless you are positively unmarried.

Time of Admission. Some homes require that you check in as early as the third month. Others will not admit you until your seventh month. You may find that on the same day one home will tell you you are too late to apply, and another will advise you that it is too early. About half of the homes discourage admission much before the sixth or seventh months. For a girl who is especially intent upon concealing the pregnancy this causes all kinds of problems. Where is she supposed to stay during the fifth (and maybe even the sixth and seventh months), when it is obvious to everyone that she is pregnant?

First Pregnancy. About ten percent of the homes will not admit a girl if it is known that she has been pregnant before. If you have been pregnant before, you may have innocently given this information as part of your medical history. Whether this is your first baby or your third you will still need maternity services. This restriction puts you on the spot, because you may either have to lie (which is not good from a medical point of view), or you may have to forgo maternity services which *should* be available to anybody who needs them.

Number of Available Adoptive Homes. A few homes limit applications according to the number of families which are available to adopt babies. This restriction automatically implies that every applicant plans to relinquish her baby for adoption, and that she has no other reason to apply to a maternity home for help. Since it is especially difficult to place babies with minority backgrounds, this restriction becomes a way of refusing admission to girls who belong to minority groups.

Religious Affiliation. Some of the Catholic homes restrict their services to girls with Catholic backgrounds. A couple of other homes restrict admission to girls of one particular faith or another, but most are somewhat flexible.

Residency. Many homes are subsidized by community funds, and the agencies are therefore reluctant to serve girls from outside the immediate area. Other homes will admit a girl who is a nonresident of the community or state only if she is able to pay the *full cost of care* and *all of her medical expenses* (which usually adds up to a minimum of $1,500). Sometimes residency restrictions depend upon a particular state's provisions for welfare and medical benefits to single, pregnant women. If you are not a U.S. citizen, you may have problems qualifying for help.

Age. Homes have various policies regarding the ages of the girls who are eligible for their services. You may have to be over sixteen or under twenty or over eighteen or under thirty. You may find that you are too old for one home and too young for another one.

The above should give you a rough idea of some of the responses you can anticipate if you decide to apply to a maternity home. Just remember that the admission requirements vary from one home to another and you should not be discouraged until you have applied at least to every home in your state.

THE PERSONAL INTERVIEW

And so now what? Assuming that you were not screened out in the process of inquiring about a home, you will probably be invited in for a personal interview with a social worker. If you live far away, you may be sent an application to fill out and return along with medical forms to be completed by your doctor. Most homes require both a proof of pregnancy and the results of tests for venereal disease before you can be admitted.

Since in a maternity home many girls live together in close quarters, an effort is made to establish some level of compatibility. This is one reason a home will request a personal interview. A member of the staff has a chance to decide whether or not you will fit in with the group; and, equally important, the interview gives you a chance to see what the home is like.

If you are considered a minor, you will probably be required to bring at least one parent to the interview. The social worker may talk to you alone for a while and then invite your parents to come in to the interview, or she may see all of you together. Sometimes it depends on the situation. If your parents insist on doing all the talking, the social worker may want an opportunity to talk to you alone. A worker will quickly notice if there is warmth and rapport between you and each of your parents or if there is tension and disagreement. Most homes are concerned with whether or not the girl herself wants to come into residence or if she is being forced against her will. At least at this level she is allowed some choice, and most homes will not accept her unless she wants to come.

Sometimes the interview involves a lot of questions about you and your family, your medical history, and facts about your national, racial, and religious origins. The same facts may also be asked about the baby's father. Or the first interview may be much more personal, focusing on the circumstances that led up to your becoming pregnant. Some workers are warm and responsive. Others may seem aloof, or you may feel that you are being forced to say things that you do not really feel.

During the first interview at a maternity home, you may suddenly find yourself fighting back the tears. This may be the first time you realize that before this is all over you are going to have a baby. You may feel like crying for a thousand other reasons, because you are scared or frustrated or embarrassed or any number of things. Do not worry about it; this is certainly an appropriate time in your life to be tearful. Crying may even help to impress the social worker with the fact that you need her. If you appear too poised and relaxed, the worker may assume that you can manage on your own when actually you have not the slightest idea where to turn.

As the interview continues, you may have a thousand questions about the home and how it operates and what you are supposed to do. Who could care less if your great-grandfather was Portuguese or Irish when you are not even sure that you ever want to see this place again? Hopefully the social worker will balance the interview so that by the end she will know a little about you and what your needs are;

you will have an impression of what this particular home is like and what you are supposed to do next.

COST

One topic that will certainly come up in the first interview is the subject of your finances and the cost of care at the home. Maternity homes are *nonprofit* organizations. None of the homes in the United States is sponsored by state or federal funds. Therefore, money has to come from somewhere to pay for rent on the building, food, staff salaries, office space, brochures, linen, heat, maintenance, and insurance. This involves thousands and thousands of dollars for each home every year.

Many homes receive a certain amount of money from community funds such as the United Crusade or the Community Chest. If the home is affiliated with a religious group, it may also receive donations from the parent organization. Local volunteer groups participate in a variety of fund-raising activities. But often these contributions still do not amount to enough money to meet the high cost of maintaining a maternity home. Most homes set an arbitrary fee for room and board on a daily or weekly basis. It usually costs a home between $1,000 and $2,000 to provide services and care for each girl, depending upon how long she remains in the home. There may be an additional cost for prenatal care, hospitalization, and delivery. Most homes determine their fees for room and board according to what it costs them to operate.

Some homes demand that the entire fee be paid by the girl and her family, possibly with help from the boy involved. A large deposit is requested at the time of admission, and the full balance is expected at the time of discharge. A few families may have no trouble parting with this much cash, but for most people it is out of the question to produce $2,000 on the spur of the moment. Consequently many homes have worked out alternative arrangements. (Others limit the people they serve to those who can afford to pay.)

At this point it would be helpful to introduce the concept of *scaled fees*. In general this means that you are asked to pay *only as much as you can*, according to your income and up to a certain maximum. The maximum is based on what it costs the home to take care of you. Let us say that you stay at a home for two months, and it costs $15 a day for room and board ($900) and $500 for all of your medical expenses. When you come in for an interview, the social worker knows that it will cost the home about $1,400 to provide you with the care and services you need. She learns from talking to you that you have only $500 to your name. When you or your parents ask, "How much is all of this going to cost?" the social worker knows that you are unable to pay the maximum $1,400. So she says, "Well, it depends . . ."

Nothing leaves people with a more uneasy feeling than being told, "It depends . . ." But if the fees are scaled, it does depend. The cost is what you can realistically afford to pay, up to a maximum of $1,400. The cost is *not* a question of how much the agency can "soak" you for. Many, many social agencies scale their fees according to each client's ability to pay, so that you will never be asked to pay more than you can afford.

Some agencies have a chart that indicates how much people should pay according to the total family budget. Some clients are able to pay the full amount and others are able to pay only a small amount, if anything. The concept of scaled fees allows people to receive services on the basis of *need*.

Once you decide to enter a maternity home, usually you and a member of the staff will decide on a total amount that seems reasonable for you to pay. You will also work out some kind of payment schedule. It may be that you pay the total amount in one lump or that you spread it out in monthly payments. Sometimes girls have no money at all during the final months of the pregnancy, but after they deliver and go back to work they are willing to pay small monthly amounts for the next year or so. As far as the maternity home is concerned, every little bit helps to stay in operation.

Sometimes the home will refer you to the local Welfare Department or to other social agencies in the community for financial aid to help meet the cost of care. Some girls reduce expenses by working in the mutual service homes mentioned earlier. Very few maternity homes offer free room and board in exchange for work performed inside the home or at an adjacent hospital, although there are many requests for this type of arrangement.

Obviously maternity care is expensive, but whether you are pregnant or not it costs somebody something to feed and shelter you wherever you are (although probably not as much). And whether your baby was planned or an accident, doctors and hospitals send out medical bills to somebody to pay for their services. Sources of income and overall expenses will be discussed in more detail in the chapter on financial resources.

ENTERING A MATERNITY HOME

If you decide to plan with a maternity home, you and the worker will set an approximate date and time for you to arrive with your suitcase in hand. In the meantime, hopefully the worker will help you make appointments with anyone else you should be seeing at this point (doctors, lawyers, teachers, adoption workers, welfare workers). If you have nowhere to stay, she may also help you to find a place until space is available at the home. Some homes provide handbooks telling you what to bring and indicating what the rules are regarding visitors, meals, mail, phone calls, and bedtime. You will probably also get an idea of what activities and programs will be available.

Most people feel a little awkward on the first day in any new or strange place, but the first day at a maternity home is especially difficult. In effect, you are going into isolation from family and friends, and you are giving up a certain amount of your freedom. For some girls it is a relief not to have to worry any more about being noticed or discovered. Tight girdles come off in exchange for loose, comfortable clothes. But still there is the newness, and the strangeness, and the uncertainty of what lies ahead.

To anyone who walks into a maternity home for the first time, it is a shock to see so many pregnant girls in one place at the same time. It takes a while to get used to it. You may be amazed at how young some of the girls are, how old some of the others are. Often the younger girls look at the older girls as if to say, "What are *you* doing here? I'm just a little kid, but you are old enough to know better!" The older girls sense this and feel all the more awkward.

PROGRAMS AND ACTIVITIES

Homes vary in the programs and activities they offer to keep the girls busy. You may be required to attend formal classes in childbirth, school subjects, and religious education. Less formal classes which may not necessarily be helpful or exciting include such subjects as typing, shorthand, piano, languages, sewing, bridge, knitting and crocheting, ceramics, painting, home crafts, and cooking.

Some homes are fairly lenient about permitting girls to go shopping or for walks during the daytime. Younger girls are usually required to obtain permission before they go anywhere. Sometimes a staff member or a volunteer will accompany a couple of girls to a movie or to the theater in the evening; a larger group of pregnant girls attracts too much attention. Volunteers may also arrange teas or picnics at their own homes so that the girls have a chance to get away for an afternoon.

Professional help includes counseling sessions with pastors, social workers, adoption workers, psychiatrists, or psychologists. Group therapy of various kinds is becoming increasingly popular at many homes. (For additional information, see the chapter on counseling and therapy.)

You will find that some homes are very rich and resourceful in what they offer to the girls, whereas others offer little more than television and monthly birthday parties. The activities are usually aimed at entertaining younger girls and may not be especially appealing to older girls who have already had a chance to be out on their own. For this reason any older girl who feels that she may be able to manage in an unsupervised setting should at least consider alternatives besides entering a maternity home.

Some homes are stricter than others about visitors and visiting hours. You may be able to continue seeing members of your family and various close friends in the afternoon and early evening. Homes have different policies about contact with young men during this period in your life even though, as one social worker pointed out, you are already pregnant.

MEDICAL CARE

Some homes may be located in the wing of a hospital, or they may be separate establishments with their own delivery rooms or nurseries. However, nowadays most of the homes have made some kind of arrangement with a nearby clinic and hospital to provide medical care for the girls.

A *few* homes will allow a girl to continue with her own doctor, or she can choose a private physician and deliver at the hospital with which he is affiliated. This becomes complicated when a maternity home is involved with a dozen doctors and hospitals with different approaches to prenatal care and attitudes toward single mothers. Consequently most homes have found it more practical and manageable to send all of the girls to one or two hospitals. The homes become familiar with the procedures at the hospitals and the staff on the maternity wards, and they can prepare the girls uniformly for what to expect when they go to the hospital.

Sometimes the girls are discharged from the hospital within twenty-four hours after delivery and are returned to a special postpartum (after delivery) section of the home to recover. Or the girl may remain in the hospital for up to five days before she returns to the home, according to the policy the home has established with the hospital. Quite a few homes (76) still have nursery facilities on the premises, so that the girl may bring her baby back to the home while further arrangements are being made. Once a girl returns from the hospital she may be required to stay at the home anywhere from three days to three weeks.

Even though the girls at a maternity home may receive their medical care elsewhere, a staff of nurses is always on hand at the home to supervise overall health care. Nurses make sure that the girls take whatever medication has been prescribed for them, and they are available to answer questions about pregnancy and symptoms of labor. The nurses may supervise diet and exercise, both of which are important during pregnancy. Girls will also be encouraged to get the rest they need. Some nurses may be quite adamant about all of this, depending upon the overall atmosphere in the home. Others are gentle and kind, and available to talk late at night when a girl may feel troubled and have difficulty getting to sleep.

More and more homes are offering classes in preparation for childbirth, which may be taught by a nurse on the staff or by a visiting public health nurse. These classes describe the basic biology of fertilization and the growth and development of the embryo. They also prepare you for what to expect during labor and delivery. The classes may also include exercises and some tips on keeping yourself clean and well-groomed. Since in most homes it will probably be assumed that you will not have sexual relations again until you are happily married, contraceptives will not be recommended or discussed.

By the time you go into labor, you will probably have been a resident at the home for at least six weeks. From the classes and clinic visits and from the tales brought back from the delivery room by other girls, you will have your own idea of what to expect when you go to the hospital.

Hospitals and maternity homes have a variety of attitudes about whether a girl who plans to give her baby up for adoption should see it, and if so, how much contact she should have with it. There are also many different opinions about whether single mothers should be mixed in with other patients in the maternity ward, or isolated (together in the regular maternity ward, but apart from the married patients), or placed in another ward entirely. Since these attitudes apply to all "unmarried mothers," whether they enter a maternity home or not, they will be discussed in more detail in the chapter on hospitalization and delivery.

As you can see, if you plan through a maternity home you will have help in making all of the arrangements that are necessary to see you through the pregnancy. But what if maternity care is not available or you prefer to make arrangements on your own? Your basic needs include room and board, money, medical care, and possibly adoption service. Younger girls and their parents may want to make special arrangements for schooling. In the chapters that follow, each of these needs will be discussed individually.

CHAPTER NINE

School programs

School systems in the United States are different from one another in their attitudes toward pregnant schoolgirls. Usually as soon as a school finds out that a girl is pregnant, she is asked to leave, even if she gets married. Some girls are probably delighted to have an excuse to drop out, but others who are eager to continue their education may find it difficult to obtain a high school diploma.

When a girl is suspended from school, she becomes inaccessible to her classmates, and they are left to their fantasies about how the pregnancy may affect her. Their own mothers become pregnant with younger brothers and sisters, but the same phenomenon is discussed in hushed whispers when it happens to a schoolgirl. Her disappearance provokes curiosity, and perhaps even respect for having done something that warrants "special" treatment.

When a girl leaves school, sometimes she can request a home teacher to help her keep up with her studies. After the baby is born, the girl must usually return to a different school. Nowadays some of the maternity homes have school programs whereby a girl may be able to study and keep up with her classmates. But often when a girl is young and pregnant and living in a strange place, it is difficult to concentrate on school work. The girls of school age in a maternity home are from many different grade levels, and they vary in their abilities, making it difficult to offer an adequate selection of classes. Many girls find it difficult to return to school after the baby is born because they feel much older and wiser, and are often no longer interested in the same things they were before the pregnancy.

In some cities where a large number of girls become pregnant and drop out of school, special school projects have been developed. To find out if such a project exists in your community, call the Unified School District or the State Board of Education. If there is a Maternity and Infant Care Project in your city (see Appendix), call and see if you are eligible for one of their programs.

The San Francisco Unified School District with the co-operation of several hospitals and agencies sponsors a program for girls who were forced to drop out of school because of pregnancy. In this program the girls continue to live at home. Two mornings a week they go to the YWCA, where each girl receives individual instruction from a teacher. By keeping up with her studies on a regular basis, the girl is more likely to feel prepared to return to school after her baby is born.

The program also offers special classes in health care and preparation for childbirth. Any pregnant girl in the district between the ages of thirteen and sixteen is encouraged to come, whether she is married or not. Counseling is available to her and her family, and a male caseworker is available for counseling with boyfriends.

Even though some schools are beginning to acknowledge responsibility for the large number of girls who drop out because of pregnancy, many pregnant schoolgirls still get lost somewhere in the system. They may be tucked out of sight at home or sent off to relatives in a neighboring state.

Either way the normal pattern of their lives is dramatically altered because of their pregnancies.

Programs such as the one mentioned above recognize the pregnant schoolgirl as someone who has the same needs as every young person in our society for education, recreation, and social activities. Because she is pregnant she has the additional needs of medical care and help in planning for her baby. She may also need help with family problems. Group counseling sessions afford her the opportunity to share her feelings with other young girls in the same situation, which can be supportive and reassuring.

Hopefully all communities will begin to sponsor comparable programs so that any girl who becomes pregnant can continue her education without interruption. Perhaps eventually schools will no longer feel it is necessary to suspend a girl simply because she is pregnant, so that whether she remains in school or drops out will be *her* decision.

CHAPTER TEN

Other living arrangements

For some girls housing is no problem. They can continue to live right where they are, or they readily find a friend or relative who will gladly take them in. For others, finding a place to stay becomes an enormous problem. If you have to leave your family home or the apartment where you have been living, think carefully about friends and relatives who are located thither and yon. Some you probably cannot stand, and others you would not want to impose on. But don't be *too* shy about asking. The person can always say no if he wants to. On the other hand, you might be just the diversion that he or she needs at this moment in his or her life, and you and your "problem" will be welcomed with enthusiasm.

If you have to leave home and you are under eighteen (or are otherwise defined as a minor), you will have to stay in a place or with a family that is licensed by the state to take care of minors. This will probably have to be a maternity home or a foster family (see page 66). Remember that depending upon your age and the fact that you are pregnant, you may be defined as a minor in one state, but not necessarily in another. Throughout the rest of this chapter it is assumed that you are legally free to establish independent residence from your family.

You could check into a hotel or the YWCA. Such an arrangement, however, is likely to become costly, since you will be obliged to eat most of your meals in restaurants. But even more important, it could be terribly bleak and lonely to stay in a hotel room all by yourself for any length of time, whether you have a suite at the Ritz or a room that looks out on a brick wall three feet away.

Perhaps the suggestions that follow will help you find a living arrangement which affords some measure of privacy but which also provides involvement with people who (you may be surprised to find) are kind and accepting of you and your situation.

WAGE HOMES OR MUTUAL SERVICE HOMES

In the chapter on maternity homes, mutual service homes or wage homes were mentioned. In these homes a pregnant girl receives room and board and perhaps a small salary in exchange for babysitting services and light housework.

Many maternity homes make arrangements for girls to stay in such homes, or sometimes a family can be located through a doctor or lawyer. Adoption agencies and other social service agencies may keep a list of families who are interested in having a pregnant girl live with them. Some girls find families through the classified pages of the newspapers or they place advertisements themselves.

The most appealing aspect of staying with a family is that you have a place to stay, and you do not have to worry where your next meal is coming from. Further advantages depend entirely upon you and the family. Some families are loving and warm and include you as one of them. They are concerned about you and your needs, just as they are concerned about one another. They will make sure that you get to all of your appointments on schedule, and they will be on hand to take you to the hospital when the time comes. You may find them generous, helpful, and supportive when you are feeling most lonely and bewildered. Girls have had wonderful experiences with families, and sometimes continue the relationship long after the baby is born.

However, this is not always the case. Most of the families who invite pregnant girls to come and live with them do not do so entirely out of the goodness of their hearts. They often say that they "would like to help a girl out," but their primary motive is to have someone come in and help with the housework and the kids. Domestic labor is increasingly expensive, along with all of the benefits that are required, transportation expenses, days off, and social security. In addition, it is increasingly difficult to find responsible and devoted people who will work for domestic wages.

And so many resourceful and busy housewives think of the pregnant girl as the perfect solution: hopefully, she will be neat and clean. She probably comes from a "decent" background or she would not be looking for a place to hide. She might even be a nice college girl. Since she will be receiving free room and board, she will not require much pay, if any. Presumably a pregnant girl does not want to go out very much because she does not want to risk running into somebody she knows, or perhaps because she has no place to go. Consequently she can be counted on to stay home most of the time. In no time "light housework" becomes scrubbing the walls and ceiling, waxing the floors, and ironing daily machine-loads of laundry while keeping an eye on five children, aged eleven and under.

It is possible that you will fall into a family that you absolutely adore, and vice versa, but you cannot count on it. Remember that just because you are pregnant is no reason why you should become somebody's slave. Pregnant or not, you are entitled to the same rewards and benefits as any other working person in this society.

Other problems may arise if you live in this type of arrangement. If you are regarded as a servant it is unlikely that you will enjoy much companionship with the family members. If you are expected to "know your place," which means to be seen and not heard, you will find yourself spending many hours by yourself or with young children, and you will miss having people your own age to be with and talk to.

Sometimes taking care of children can help you to decide whether or not you want to keep your baby. If you have already decided to keep your baby, taking care of somebody else's child is excellent preparation. However, if you feel compelled to give up your baby, you may find it difficult to take care of somebody else's children at this time.

Some girls are certain from the beginning that they are going to keep their babies, while others are equally certain that they are going to give them up. Many girls go back and forth in the decision to keep or relinquish, and the months before delivery become anguished days of indecision. This period may be difficult enough due to pressure from your own family. But add to this the involvement of the family you are staying with. (Even professionals in the field have trouble remaining objective about whether a girl should keep or give up her baby.) Many families, by advising you according to what *they* would do, make it even more difficult for you to act on your own decision about what to do with the baby.

BOARDING HOUSES

If you have a little cash to support yourself through the pregnancy, you may consider living in a boarding house. Most boarding houses accommodate up to ten people at a time. You may have a private room (which will cost more) or share with one or two other people. Of course you will share the bathroom, living room, kitchen, and any other community rooms with the other residents in the house.

Most boarding houses serve breakfast and dinner at fixed mealtimes, and the cost is included in the weekly rate, which probably begins at about $35. The amount may be slightly less if you reserve your room by the month. (Prices vary from one section of the country to another.) A few boarding houses allow the guests the freedom to use the kitchen to prepare their own meals. Some boarding houses are exclusively for men and women; others are for both. Some cater to religious or ethnic groups and discriminate on that basis. A black girl will probably have even more trouble getting into a boarding house than she may have getting into a maternity home.

Usually at a boarding house people come and go throughout the day so that you would not be left alone for long periods at a time. Many of the houses are quite small and have a friendly, family atmosphere.

RESIDENCE CLUBS

Some cities have residence clubs, which are similar to boarding houses except that they accommodate a larger number of people. They are perfect for newcomers who do not want to (or who cannot afford to) settle in an apartment until they have found jobs. Many people stay in residence clubs until they become acquainted with one or two others who are interested in sharing an apartment. The rates, which are about $135 minimum per month, usually include two meals a day. Some are exclusively for men or women, while others include both sexes.

Considering that you may be self-conscious about the fact that you are pregnant, you can save yourself a lot of embarrassment by using the telephone. Both boarding houses and residence clubs are listed under "Boarding Houses" in the

Yellow Pages of your telephone book. If they are not, check for the correct listing in the Index to the phone book (sometimes called the Blue Pages) or call Information. You might also glance over the classified section of the newspapers. When you phone, ask if they have any vacancies, what their rates are, and if they accept pregnant girls. Even if they say no but you are not visibly pregnant, you can still go there until you have a chance to make other arrangements. You might even find someone else in the same predicament who would be delighted to share an apartment.

APARTMENTS

Generally apartments are not very economical unless you move in with someone else who is already established. The following will give you an idea of the problems you may have in finding a place to live:

1. Many landlords require a full-year lease with first and last months' rent paid in advance. (What if you only plan to be in town for three or four months?) If the rent is $145 a month (for a two-bedroom apartment for four girls), this means $290 to begin with, in cash!

2. In addition, you can count on a $35 to $75 (often nonrefundable) cleaning deposit.

3. Even if you promise the landlord that full rent will be paid on time, he may look skeptically at anyone who is unemployed.

4. Some landlords accept only older people. Others rent only to couples. If you say that your "husband" will be joining you shortly, you may then be told that there are to be no children in the building.

5. Many managers discriminate against minority groups.

6. If you will be staying only briefly in the area, you

will probably look mostly at furnished apartments. This still leaves the problem of investing in linens and kitchen utensils.

7. Since you should have access to immediate medical care, it is a good idea to have a telephone installed. This means another $25 in cash toward a deposit for telephone service.

8. If you get together with other girls in the same situation, even if you know and like each other when you first move into an apartment, you may still find it difficult to coordinate meals, grocery shopping, and finances in general. There may also be a fairly constant turnover as you seek out "new" girls to replace the "old" ones who deliver their babies and move on. A variety of problems may be created when roommates decide to keep their babies and bring them back to the apartment from the hospital. *Any* problem will be intensified by the fact that there is nowhere else to go if the situation becomes intolerable.

If you decide that you want to live in an apartment and have the necessary funds and equipment, there are three basic approaches to looking for one. You can check the ads in the newspaper, or list yourself with a realtor (who may or may not charge a fee), or wander around in a neighborhood you like and look for "For Rent" signs. Apartment hunting in a city is generally tedious and exhausting. Invariably you start out with a picture in your head of the delightful little place you are going to find. After looking at a couple of places you begin to realize that such a place does not exist (or if it ̄ ̄ it probably costs at least $400 a month). Do not be- ̄ ̄ ̄raged *too* fast, and do not decide that you are ̄ ̄ d away because you are pregnant. Landlords have

CHAPTER TWELVE

Medical care

So far in this book we have focused exclusively on *you* as an individual with a particular kind of problem. Often in its earlier stages an unexpected pregnancy is regarded as a "disease" which hopefully can be gotten rid of before it causes too much social and physical discomfort. However, as time passes, you begin to realize that this is not just a "condition" you are dealing with. The outcome of all of this will be a baby. It is important for you to be healthy during this experience, and happy too, if that is possible. But from now on we have to take your baby into consideration because we want him to be healthy too.

WHY MEDICAL CARE IS IMPORTANT

Medical science has proved that a woman's diet and overall health during pregnancy influence the growth and development of the baby inside her. The average woman should carry a baby for nine months, or about forty weeks. Because prematurity accounts for so many deaths and crippling defects in babies, a considerable amount of research has gone into determining its causes. Poor diet has been found to be one cause. Another cause is from having babies so close together that the mother's body does not have a chance to rest and recover in between. (This may not apply to you now, but it is something to bear in mind for the future.)

Even though premature babies may appear healthy and whole, they are often sick and have to be kept in incubators under intensive care in the hospital nursery. Because they are born early, they are *not finished* when they arrive. Their bodies are not ready to handle all of the intricacies of eating and breathing that we take for granted. The word *premature* means *before* something is *ripe* or *ready*. Sometimes with the aid of medical technology, the baby can continue to develop and grow outside of his mother's body. But all too often the developmental process has been interrupted in such a way that the baby either dies or is handicapped in any number of ways.

Premature births are mentioned not to frighten you but to emphasize the importance of taking care of yourself while you are pregnant. You must have responsible medical care during your pregnancy, even though it may be difficult to come by.

WHERE TO GO FOR MEDICAL CARE

Possibly you know of a particular doctor whom you would like throughout prenatal care and delivery. If you are at all frightened or concerned about the pregnancy, it can be reassuring to have a doctor whom you like and trust. If you feel that a doctor is not treating you as kindly as he is his other patients *only* because you are not married, ask him about it. A frank discussion might be useful to both of you. Otherwise switch to someone who is more understanding and accepting.

Medical care is available through several different sources. Private physicians have their offices alone or in small groups with other doctors. Private medical care often costs more than other kinds of medical arrangements, but you may be eligible for Medicaid. (See page 100.) For prenatal care, hospitalization, and delivery, it is unlikely that the cost will be less than $500, and it may be considerably more. It is a good idea to be very clear about how much you are expected to pay from the very beginning.

A doctor may offer to arrange for a family to pay your medical expenses if you are willing to let them adopt your baby. (This is discussed in more detail in the chapter on adoption.) However, under no circumstances should you allow yourself to feel trapped into such an agreement.

If you find the cost of private medical care prohibitive, or if it is difficult to find a doctor you like, you might consider some of the public facilities which offer medical care. These include the county hospitals and various university clinics and hospitals. For information about these, call the local Medical Society.

Clinics vary in their purpose and style, but after one or two visits you may meet a doctor you like who will follow through with you as long as your appointments are scheduled when he is on duty. As you become familiar with the clinic and the procedures there, you will learn what to expect when it is time for you to deliver. In some ways you may be better informed about the hospital and its delivery-room practices than many of the private patients who never visit the hospital until they go into labor.

If you qualify as a military dependent, you can register at an army or navy hospital for complete medical services.

In Chapter Four, which describes a variety of places you can go for different kinds of services, reference is made to the Maternity and Infant Care projects that are located in different cities in the United States. A complete list of these is offered on pages 209–215 in the Appendix. If there is a project in your area, members of the staff will direct you to the appropriate source for medical care.

At the time of your first prenatal visit, you will usually be given a complete physical examination. Samples of your blood and urine will be sent to a laboratory for testing. The doctor will take measurements of your abdomen and pelvis so that he can follow the growth of the baby in the months to come. Subsequent visits are usually briefer, depending upon how far along you are in the pregnancy and whether or not suspicious symptoms develop along the way.

Many women develop problems with their teeth during pregnancy. If you begin to notice any discomfort, it is advisable to see a dentist in spite of the expense. Medical insurance or Medicaid may also include dental care.

PHYSICAL CHANGES DURING PREGNANCY

Since this chapter is focused on the medical aspects of pregnancy, you may want some idea of how you will feel and what you can expect as the pregnancy continues.

At the beginning you may notice nothing more than the absence of regular menstrual periods, but various changes are beginning to take place inside you. By the end of the first month (the fourth week), the embryo is little more than a mass of flesh. By the end of the fourth month the embryo resembles a fully formed baby. He even has finger nails and eyelashes.

Probably your breasts will get bigger, and feel tender. Occasionally they may secrete a fluid which is the result of glandular tissue changes that enable you to produce milk. You may also notice an increase in vaginal discharge, which may become profuse and thick and itchy. Many girls are mortified, suspecting that they have acquired a venereal disease along with becoming pregnant. Usually the discharge is symptomatic of a rather common vaginal infection. By all means mention it to your doctor so that he can give you something to clear it up and relieve the itching.

For most women the pregnancy begins to show during the fifth month. You may notice stretch marks on your breasts and abdomen. These marks become increasingly apparent as the pregnancy advances, but depending on the elasticity of your skin they will probably fade or even vanish after delivery. Many women have the same marks from gaining and losing weight, without ever having been pregnant.

In the midst of all of this, usually sometime during the fifth month, you will begin to feel the baby move. The medical term for this is "quickening." At first you may confuse it with gas, but this feeling does not pass like gas. Eventually the feeling becomes unmistakable, and from then on you will know when your baby is awake or resting. You may feel your baby hiccough or sneeze or do other things too.

Some women hardly notice any changes at all during pregnancy, while others become so uncomfortable or weepy or fatigued that they can hardly function. These are some of the common complaints that pregnant women have:

Heartburn
Too much saliva in the mouth
Frequent urination
Constipation
A lot of gas
Hemorrhoids (varicose veins in the rectal area)
Varicose veins
Nosebleeds and nasal congestion
Leg cramps
Swelling of the ankles and legs
Painful contractions of the uterus
Faintness
Backache
Trouble sleeping
Shortness of breath

Moodiness (tearfulness, irritability)

Changes in the color and complexion of the skin (some women develop pregnancy masks; a few develop blemishes; others find that their skin clears up for the first time in years)

The above indicate some of the reactions you may have to the dramatic changes that are taking place in your body as the pregnancy continues. If you mention whatever problems you are having to your doctor, he may be able to suggest ways of reducing some of the discomfort. Often it is wise to consult him before you apply home remedies of your own.

Danger Signs

Some symptoms are definite warning signals that something is going wrong. These symptoms may occur at any time during your pregnancy. If they do, call a doctor immediately and follow his instructions carefully. Even if you would *like* to lose the baby, remember that your own health may be at stake. The following symptoms indicate what may be serious hazards to you or to the baby or to both of you:

Vaginal bleeding or hemorrhaging

Puffiness of the face, eyes, or fingers, especially if this occurs very suddenly

Severe, unremitting headache

Dimness or blurring of vision

Severe abdominal pain

Frequent vomiting

Fever over 100° F.

Rupture of the membranes resulting in the escape of watery fluid from the vagina

Absence of fetal movements for twenty-four hours, from the thirtieth week on

DIET AND DRUGS

In order to remain healthy and comfortable during pregnancy it is a good idea to watch what you eat. A healthy diet for most people in this culture consists of meat, vegetables, and fruit. Some pregnant women are encouraged to drink milk; others are advised to exclude it from their diets entirely. Doctors will generally recommend vitamins and iron pills to supplement a woman's regular diet. Rich and fatty foods are discouraged. Women who are poorly nourished are inclined to have premature babies. If the mother's body is starving, she cannot tolerate the increasing demands of the baby growing inside her and her body has to get rid of the baby.

Salt intake must be limited during pregnancy or the body will retain fluids, causing legs and ankles to become puffy. This condition is called edema. Too much salt can eventually lead to a condition called toxemia, a quick and sudden weight gain which occurs most often in late pregnancy. Toxemia must be treated immediately, since it can become a matter of life and death to the mother and child. Although it can be controlled, it will not go away until after delivery.

Quite often during pregnancy women appear to have a high sugar count like that associated with diabetes, but this symptom usually disappears immediately after delivery.

As you probably know, during pregnancy the baby is fed via the placenta through the umbilical cord which conducts materials back and forth from the mother's system. Consequently the mother must be cautious about what she eats or takes into her system by injection. Generally what is harmful for the mother will also be harmful for the baby, but the reverse is not necessarily true. Some things which are not so harmful to the mother, can be very damaging to the baby. This is true of certain kinds of drugs. One example is thalidomide, a drug prescribed as a tranquilizer which turned out to affect the development of the embryo during early pregnancy, producing gross malformations in many of the babies that were subsequently born. Even aspirin in large amounts is not especially good for your baby. It is wise to consult your doctor before taking any medication or treatment in case it might be harmful.

Doctors are becoming more and more familiar with the symptoms of drug addiction in newborns. Addiction occurs as a result of the mother's use of narcotics during the pregnancy. As soon as the baby is born, he must be treated for withdrawal like any adult addict. A possible relationship between LSD and various birth defects has been suggested, but too little evidence is available to make an arbitrary statement about the chemical effects of LSD on unborn babies. Certainly the fact that there is a possible connection warrants caution. Also, you do not always know what you are getting when you take LSD or other hallucinogens, and without realizing it you might take some other substance which is definitely damaging to your baby.

There is no scientific evidence to discourage the use of marijuana during pregnancy, but during labor the drug slows down the contractions (one of the reasons why anesthesia is not administered until late in labor), and has to wear off before they will start up again.

FEELING COMFORTABLE AND ATTRACTIVE

If you are trying to hide the pregnancy, you will probably feel miserable for as long as you have to cram yourself into clothes that do not fit. As styles vary, this is not always such a major problem. Naturally you will feel most comfortable in things that fit loosely. You can purchase brassieres and girdles that are made especially for pregnant women at department stores and maternity shops. Many women, married or otherwise, begin to feel fat and ugly and they abandon all efforts at looking fresh and attractive. Other women are radiant and more beautiful than ever when they are pregnant. Some of this may have to do with the mood shifts that accompany pregnancy. Maybe if you fuss over yourself a little bit, you will feel better.

MOOD SHIFTS

Many women are especially moody right before their menstrual periods. They may feel full of energy, almost frantic, or jittery and tearful. This behavior is attributed to shifts in the hormonal balance during the course of a woman's monthly cycle. Similar shifts take place during pregnancy. If a woman is married, people are inclined to be understanding, and they dismiss various outbursts as something to be expected. If a girl is single, however, when she appears moody or depressed, people are quick to assume that she is unhappy because of her situation. Often pregnant girls themselves feel as if they have lost control of their emotions, when they are only reacting like most pregnant women to the biological changes that are taking place in their bodies.

REST AND AMUSEMENT

If you are employed, you may find it increasingly difficult to continue through the day without becoming completely exhausted. Ideally, if you do become fatigued you should take a nap during the afternoon. If you are not employed, you may get too much rest and have difficulty finding things to do to keep busy.

You may find that you finally have a chance to read all of those books you have been wanting to get to for months, but it is difficult to get involved in them when that is *all* you have to do. You may have all kinds of hobbies, but because of your financial situation you cannot afford the materials involved.

Many girls, inhibited by the pregnancy, find this to be one time in their lives when they are not especially eager to meet people. If you can get past that feeling, there are a lot of things you can do to pass the time.

For example, call the city Volunteer Bureau (almost any social agency should be able to give you the address and phone number). Perhaps you will be asked to spend several hours a week reading to a blind person, or keeping an eye on children in a nursery school. Volunteers are used in many settings, and some of them might be quite interesting. If you leave a notice in the laundry or on the board at the neighborhood grocery store (assuming there is one), you may be able to get part-time work babysitting or sewing or ironing. Perhaps you have a talent that you could put to work, such as sketching, or tutoring in a language, or teaching piano, or folk dancing.

In every city there are many kinds of daytime and evening classes. Some cost money, for example if you decided to study a language at Berlitz. But many classes are free or cost only a nominal enrollment fee. For information call the department of adult education at various high schools and colleges. This may be a good chance to learn typing, shorthand, pottery, Spanish, or sewing. In most yarn shops someone is available to teach you to knit or crochet. You can also call recreation centers like the YWCA and the Jewish Community Center to find out if classes are being offered in activities such as bridge and swimming.

It is important to keep busy. If you are inclined to feel depressed, there is nothing worse than feeling that you are useless and that your life is slipping by. Of course this experience will be over in time, but as you go through it from day to day, it can seem like forever. Along with having places to go and something to do, goes being with people, getting outside in the (fresh?) air, exercise—all of the things that are the fabric and substance of life anyway.

TRAVEL

Women sometimes wonder if it is safe to travel during pregnancy. The greatest hazard lies in traveling late in pregnancy. For one thing it is uncomfortable to sit without changing your position for many hours at a time. You should make a point of getting up and moving about at regular intervals. If it is at all possible, you should keep your legs up to aid circulation. Naturally it is awkward if you go into premature labor far from medical services of any kind. Many transportation companies, in order to protect their drivers and pilots from performing the duties of a midwife, require a written statement from a doctor before they will issue a ticket to a woman who is beyond a certain point in pregnancy. This is for her protection as well as theirs.

SEXUAL RELATIONS

Many girls wonder about having sexual relations during pregnancy, but they are afraid to ask, just as they are afraid to ask about drugs or venereal disease. Most doctors will tell you that it is all right to have intercourse up until four weeks before delivery, but many people continue to have relations throughout without any ill effects. However, if you notice any bleeding following intercourse, something might be wrong and it is wise to call your doctor. Most doctors will advise you to avoid intercourse for one month after delivery because of the high risk of infection.

CLASSES IN CHILDBIRTH

Many clinics and maternity homes offer formal classes as preparation for childbirth. In the past, women knew very little about pregnancy and childbirth, and they accepted the baby, when he arrived, as something of a miracle. The total experience was generally shrouded in mystery and fear. In recent years doctors have found that women are much less frightened, especially during labor and delivery, if they understand what is going on. When a woman is afraid, she fights the pain, which only makes it worse. If she recognizes the changes as they are taking place in her body, she is more likely to relax, and the pain is not as severe.

Childbirth classes are conducted by nurses or other qualified persons. A series usually consists of eight classes which meet once a week. The classes begin with a discussion of menstruation and the fertilization process. They continue with a description of the growth and development of the baby, along with the corresponding changes that occur in the woman's body. The classes also include a discussion of nutrition, exercise, and other aspects of health care. One or two films may be shown which illustrate what happens during delivery.

The classes can be helpful in many ways. When you go to the doctor you may have questions that you either forget or are too embarrassed to ask. The doctor may be rushed, or he may fail to explain something that you do not understand at all. A great number of questions will automatically be answered in the classes. Also, it is reassuring to know that other pregnant women have many of the same questions and worries that you have.

By the time you have completed the classes, you will know what the signs are for early labor, how to time your contractions, and when to call the hospital. You will know what to expect when you are admitted to the labor room, how to breathe to make the contractions less painful, and the different anesthetics you can choose from. Finally, you will be familiar with the procedures in the delivery room, and with the instruments and how they are used. The more you know about the entire process, the easier it will be for both you and the baby.

Childbirth classes are offered by a number of different organizations. They are usually free. Contact any of the following for more information:

Public Health Department
Red Cross
YWCA
Maternity homes
Welfare Department
Local hospitals and churches

These places may also be able to advise you about classes (or books) in natural childbirth, if you are interested.

If you plan to keep your baby, it is a good idea to inquire about classes in child care as well.

VENEREAL DISEASES

When we talk about venereal diseases we are usually referring to syphilis and gonorrhea. Both are extremely contagious and are transmitted by intimate sexual contact. Although we most often associate venereal diseases with the genital regions, the mouth and anus are not entirely immune.

Because VD is transmitted via sexual contact, we run into many of the same problems of embarrassment and shock that are associated with out-of-wedlock pregnancy or with abortion. This is unfortunate because venereal diseases are no different from any other infection that can be treated with antibiotics.

Venereal diseases can be cured if they are diagnosed and treated early. They *must* be treated. They will *not* go away by themselves. If they are allowed to spread in your body, they can cause irreparable damage. Also, they are highly contagious. This is why it is so important to seek treatment, no matter how embarrassing it may be, if there is *any* possibility that you have been exposed to syphilis or gonorrhea.

If you notice a vaginal discharge or an unusual sore in your genital area, these *could* be symptoms of VD (many girls are too embarrassed to ask their doctors), but they could just as easily be normal symptoms of pregnancy. On the other hand, you may have VD without showing any symptoms. Many women are carriers without realizing it until a man complains that he has been infected.

Blood tests are given to determine whether or not a person has syphilis. In most states your blood will automatically be tested for this at the time of your first prenatal visit. To test for gonorrhea a small sample of the secretion in your vagina is used, but this test will probably not be performed unless you request it.

Today VD is so common that many, many people get it. It is by no means limited to sailors and prostitutes. If you have any questions about it but prefer not to contact your own doctor, call the Public Health Department or a Planned Parenthood agency for more information. Either one of these places may have clinic facilities where you can be tested and treated.

A law was recently passed in the state of California making it possible for anyone over the age of *twelve* to go to a clinic and receive medical care for any communicable disease. This, of course, includes venereal diseases. This law spares a young person from confessing the details of his sexual activities to his parents in order to obtain the medical care he may urgently require. Many parents in the United States today are simply not prepared to deal with the consequences of their children's activities and interests, especially if the children are involved in sexual relations and drug use. When a young person needs medical care, he or she should have immediate and direct access to it regardless of whether he has a good or poor relationship with his parents.

CHAPTER THIRTEEN

Adoption

As you continue through the pregnancy, you will become increasingly aware of the baby inside you, and if you have not given it much thought before, it might be a good idea to consider what you are going to do with him when he gets here. There are several alternatives.

First of all, you can keep him and take care of him with the help of whatever relatives, friends, and resources are available to you. In recent years more and more girls are finding it possible to do this. Certainly numerous problems exist, but gradually society is becoming more accepting of single mothers who keep their babies. By now many single women are rearing children. They may be divorced, separated, widowed, or unmarried. In many ways the circumstances do not make a great deal of difference. On a day-to-day basis the challenges and the responsibilities of a single parent are much the same.

It is always easier if you have family, friends, or a boyfriend to offer encouragement and moral support. The presence or absence of financial problems can also make a great deal of difference. As some communities recognize the pressures on single mothers, services are being developed to lighten their burdens. For more information about these services see Chapter Seventeen.

A second alternative is to give the baby up for adoption. Different kinds of adoption will be discussed in this chapter.

Finally, you can place the baby temporarily, either with your family or with friends or in foster care, until you are able to take over the full care of your child yourself. This alternative will be discussed at the end of this chapter. (If you do leave your baby with people who are not directly related to you, make sure that you have applied for a legal transfer of custody through a lawyer or child welfare agency. Otherwise these people cannot authorize permission for medical care or any other service in an emergency. It may be tempting to drop your baby into someone else's lap and run, but this may lead to very unfortunate consequences for your baby.)

If you are considering adoption, it is important for you to know what adoption is and what the procedures are. The adoption process is not especially complicated, but you must be sufficiently well informed so that you are assured that both you and your baby are legally protected. Also, people have a lot of misconceptions about adoption which are based on isolated incidents. In the pages that follow you will find a description of the two kinds of legal adoption that exist and a discussion of some of the advantages and disadvantages of each.

When you relinquish a baby for adoption, it means that you give up all of your legal rights as parent of the child to somebody else. Once all of the procedures are completed, the decision is irreversible, and very, very rarely can you get your baby back. This is why it is *so* important for you to know what you are doing when you sign consent or relinquishment papers. For your protection, these papers can never be signed until *after* the baby is born.

As the natural mother of a baby, you are absolutely the only person who can decide to give your baby up.* Other people can threaten you and put pressure on you, but legally the baby is yours until *you* sign papers stating otherwise. In some states, depending upon your age, the signature of your parent or guardian may also be required, but no one can sign your baby away without your consent. Many girls are afraid that the baby's father will try to take the baby away, but he is like anyone else, and he has no right to take or to have the baby without your permission.

Occasionally a woman can be proven to be incompetent to make a decision. This might apply if she is in a mental hospital or if she is severely retarded. Whatever the situation, the matter must be brought before a court, and substantial evidence presented to show that a woman is incapable or incompetent to make a decision about the future of her child. If the court feels that the woman is only temporarily incompetent to make the decision, it will allow a reasonable time for her to recover, so that if at all possible the decision will be hers and not somebody else's.

TYPES OF ADOPTION

The two kinds of legal adoption, *agency* adoption and *independent* adoption (also referred to as private adoption), will be discussed in detail. The procedures for relative adoption,

---

* The only exception to this is if a woman is married. No matter who the baby's father really is, her husband is the legal father of the child, even if she has not seen him for a couple of years. A woman's husband is considered the legal father of the child if the child is born up to 300 days after a final decree for divorce has been issued, and she cannot relinquish the baby for adoption without her husband's consent. If you find yourself in this situation, consult a lawyer as soon as possible.

which occurs when you place the baby with relatives or possibly with friends, are the same as the procedures for independent adoption. This is an ideal solution for some girls because they can watch their babies grow and develop even though they are not ready to assume the full responsibility of parenthood. The problems which can arise as a result of this type of arrangement will also be discussed further on.

Agency Adoption

Most social workers will advise a girl to seek adoption service through an agency. Some agencies are a part of the state Department of Social Welfare (possibly listed under Child Welfare). Others are independent, nonsectarian agencies like the Children's Home Society in California or the Boston Children's Service in Massachusetts. A number of private agencies are administered by various religious organizations, and a few maternity homes are still licensed to offer adoption service.

Even though an effort has been made to set standards for adoption practices in licensed agencies, individual agencies and adoption workers differ greatly in their attitudes toward the natural mother and what they consider to be in her best interest. They also vary in what they consider best for the baby and in how they define standards for good adopting parents. These differences will become apparent as we continue. In the meantime, here is a general idea of how agency adoption works, theoretically:

A pregnant girl who thinks she wants to give up her baby for adoption calls an agency and makes an appointment with a social worker. She will not be offered an appointment unless the agency feels confident that it can place her baby in a permanent home; this is one reason why it is important to apply for adoption service as early as possible. It will be especially difficult for girls with racially mixed babies to find an agency that will accept them. Many girls are turned away from adoption agencies because the quota for babies has been filled, or because there is insufficient staff to process more applications.

Assuming that an initial appointment has been offered, the girl and the social worker will meet several times in the next few months before the baby is born. During this period the social worker collects as much information as she can about the girl and her family background, and about the baby's father and his family background if the information is available. These questions are in no way meant as a test. They give the worker an idea of what the baby will be like when he is born and as he grows up so that he can be placed with parents who seem appropriate. Important concerns are physical appearance, religious affiliations, and hereditary health problems. As the worker becomes acquainted with the girl, she also gets some feeling of how the girl would rear the baby if she were able to keep him herself.

During these interviews the social worker also discusses with the girl the adoption process and how it works. Hopefully, she gives the girl an opportunity to raise whatever questions she has about adoption and to express her reactions, whatever they may be. In applying to an adoption agency, a girl in no way obligates herself to give up her baby. The worker should be helpful to the girl in working toward a decision, but she should never be coercive. After the baby is born, the worker should continue to be available in a supportive capacity until a final decision has been reached. A good adoption worker will help a girl to arrive at the decision that seems best for the girl and her baby. If the girl decides to keep her baby, the worker will make sure that she is referred to appropriate agencies which offer ongoing services, according to the mother's needs.

If after the baby is born the girl still wants to relinquish her baby for adoption, arrangements will be made by the agency to take the baby from the hospital and to place him in a temporary home. (Variations in procedures will be discussed more fully in the chapter on hospitalization and delivery.) These are usually small private homes retained by the agency to receive and care for newborn babies until further arrangements have been made. The natural mother has the opportunity to leave the hospital and to get back on her feet after delivery before she makes a final, irrevocable decision about her child. Only in very rare instances should an agency permit a girl to sign final papers before she has left the hospital.

During this interim period the agency has the baby examined by staff doctors to determine his overall state of health. If anything appears to be seriously wrong with the baby, the agency will try to find a family that is prepared to take care of him, depending upon his particular problem.

The period of time varies, but most agencies like to have the final papers signed sometime between two and six weeks after delivery, so that the baby can be placed in a permanent home as quickly as possible. A baby is never placed with adopting parents *before* the papers are signed. If the natural mother decides that she wants to keep her baby after all, it means that no one has been hurt or disappointed by her change of mind.

When an agency is involved, the natural mother relinquishes full legal custody of her baby to the agency. It becomes the agency's responsibility to place the child in a suitable home. For this reason agencies are reluctant to accept more applications from natural mothers than they can accommodate. In some states, even though the natural mother has signed the final papers she may still be held responsible for the child until he has been placed with a family.

Some babies are placed immediately. In other instances

there may be a delay in finding the right family for a particular child. A natural mother is welcome to remain in touch with the agency until she is satisfied that her child has been placed in a permanent home. Usually the agency will share with the natural mother some information about the family such as the age of the parents, the father's occupation, whether there are other children in the family, and recreational preferences. However, the agency does not reveal the name and address of the family, partly to spare the natural mother from the temptation to seek out or claim her child as the years go by. Nor does the agency reveal to the adopting parents more than very general information about the natural mother. This protects the natural mother from the fear that she may one day have an unexpected visit from the child she gave up for adoption many years before.

As soon as the baby is born and while the natural mother is still in the hospital, she fills out a birth certificate with as much information as she is willing to give about herself and the baby's father. (Much of this information is used only for statistical purposes.) The birth certificate is kept with all of the other papers related to the adoption. When the baby is placed, a second birth certificate is filled out for the adopting couple as if the wife had gone to the hospital and had given birth to the child herself. When the adoption is final, the original birth certificate is sealed in a vault. It can be opened in rare instances, only as a result of a petition filed by an attorney for what is considered to be a good reason.

No fees are ever paid to the agency by the natural mother. The service is paid for by fees collected from the adopting parents and often by contributions from other community resources.

While pregnant girls are being interviewed, families are also calling the agency to find out how they can adopt a baby. A social worker is assigned to work with each couple, and interviews are scheduled to discuss the family's interest in adopting a child and the procedures involved. Both husband and wife are asked questions about physical traits within their families, their religious affiliations, their financial situation, and health problems.

The interviews with prospective parents are much more rigorous than the ones with the natural mothers. For them the experience is like a test which they can either pass or fail. If the couple has no children of their own, the social worker wants to know why and how they have dealt with this problem. Does one partner blame the other? Whose idea was it to adopt? Are both equally enthusiastic about the idea? And so on.

The social worker probes into the couple's educational background, their employment history, their social life, their sense of civic responsibility, and the amount of their church participation. Usually the social worker visits their home at least once, and before she can approve them for adoption she must see the results of complete medical checkups. Once the couple is approved, they are eligible to receive the next suitable baby who is released to the agency by the natural mother. The screening process usually takes somewhere between six months to a year. Many couples drop out or are disqualified along the way.

Independent Adoption

In an independent adoption, instead of using an agency as an informed intermediary for placing the child, the mother assumes responsibility for placing the child herself, either with relatives or friends, or with a family who has been referred by a doctor or lawyer or some other person with whom she has had contact during the pregnancy. Most social workers will advise against independent (also referred to as private) adoptions. They are commonly practiced in most states, although in some states it is illegal to relinquish a baby to anyone other than a blood relative (or of course to a licensed agency). The procedures for independent adoption are much less structured than they are in agency adoption, and they are therefore more susceptible to legal oversights that can cause problems for everyone involved. In general, independent adoption places a greater responsibility on the natural mother to know and to exercise her rights as the legal mother of her child. However, these placements often can and do work out successfully.

Independent adoptions vary according to circumstances and the people involved. However, this is an example of a fairly common independent adoption arrangement:

A young woman goes to an obstetrician-gynecologist to find out if she is pregnant. It turns out that she is, and as she and the doctor discuss the alternatives for what she can do, the doctor mentions that he knows of a very nice couple who is looking for a baby to adopt. Often lawyers also know of such couples. The doctor contacts the couple, and if they are interested they usually agree to pay all, or at least a part, of the girl's medical expenses. This can be helpful to a pregnant girl if she has a limited source of income.

The doctor may ask the young woman if she would like to meet the couple to see if she approves of them as parents for her child. He may also refer her to a lawyer to make sure that proper papers are filed as the procedure progresses.

The girl may or may not meet the couple depending upon how she feels about the situation. If she does meet them, she has to decide for herself if they will be suitable parents. If she does not meet them, she has to rely on the word of the doctor, whose chief interest may be in matching supply and demand.

When the baby is born, the couple takes him directly home from the hospital. This is often considered the outstanding advantage of independent adoption. If all goes smoothly, indeed it is ideal for the baby to go directly into a home with parents who have chosen to love him and take care of him. In the ensuing months the papers are processed, and within six months to a year adoption is final, to everyone's relief and satisfaction.

But things do not always go so smoothly. In an independent adoption there is no protection against the possibility that one of the parties involved might change his or her mind. Legally, anyone can back out of the agreement for any reason up until the final papers are signed, which may be anywhere from six months to a year after the baby is born. Sometimes the wife becomes pregnant with her own child, or the husband has a heart attack, or the couple decides to get a divorce. If for any reason the couple loses interest in adopting the baby, the natural mother is suddenly left with her baby and possibly unpaid medical bills as well.

It is one thing if the adoption falls through *before* the baby is born. Maybe another couple can still be found. But what if the problems arise *after* the baby is born? If the couple want to return the baby, what is the young woman supposed to do? If something is wrong with the baby, and the couple refuses the child, the situation can be especially unfortunate.

More and more often girls change their minds and decide to keep their babies after they are born. A girl has every right to decide to keep her baby, but what does she do about her sense of obligation and commitment to the couple? The original understanding was that she would surrender the baby to them at birth, and at the time she was grateful that they were available to take the problem off her hands. But if circumstances change, and if the natural mother decides to keep her baby, what about the disappointed couple?

In an independent adoption, the couple must be approved by the state Department of Social Welfare before the final papers can be signed. The criteria are quite relaxed compared to the careful screening that takes place when a couple applies for a baby through an agency. Even so, some couples fail to pass the basic requirements, and again the responsibility falls back onto the natural mother to find another family for her child.

Besides waiting for an investigation by the state Department of Social Welfare, there may be other delays related to court procedures. As long as both parties are consistently pleased with the adoption arrangement there is no problem. But if a change of heart arises on either side, the fact that the procedures are incomplete leaves both parties vulnerable.

A specific legal procedure must be followed in each state to complete an independent adoption. It is important to realize that an incomplete or improperly filed adoption petition can leave a child in legal limbo. In some cases the natural mother may never know that something went wrong in the legal process. For up to five years after the adoption decree has been granted, the papers can be contested in a court of law, and unless they have been properly processed from beginning to end, they can be invalidated.

If you are involved in independent adoption proceedings, it is wise to select an attorney who has experience in handling adoptions. Some lawyers prepare such papers regularly. For others it is less of a specialty, and if they are not familiar with the procedures they may leave loopholes which can be questioned or challenged later on.

As was mentioned at the beginning of this chapter, adoption cannot take place *unless* the natural mother has signed papers relinquishing all of her legal rights as a natural parent of the child *to* somebody else. In the case of an independent adoption she signs a *consent*, which indicates her approval of a particular couple as the adopting parents of her child. If she leaves town or disappears without having signed such a consent, her baby is not free to be adopted. The couple involved has to go to great lengths to prove that the natural mother has *abandoned* the child for at least one year, sometimes longer, before they can petition to adopt. In the meantime, they have to live with the fear that the natural mother may return at any time and claim her child, which occasionally happens. This interferes with the formation of a secure parent-child relationship, which can be so critical during the early months and years of a child's life.

Relative Adoption

Relative adoption is a form of independent adoption in which the natural mother relinquishes her legal rights as mother of the child to someone else in the family. It also applies when, for example, a stepfather adopts his wife's children or vice versa. Sometimes when a mother is very young, her parents adopt the baby and rear it as a younger brother or sister. Sometimes the baby is surrendered to a childless aunt and uncle or to a sister and brother-in-law. If no papers are filed, the natural mother can claim legal custody of her child at any time. The couple, even though they are relatives, may be reluctant to part with the child, and all kinds of problems may ensue.

In the case of either an independent or a relative adoption, the natural mother often meets the adopting couple. They may meet only once or twice and never see each other again after the adoption is final. On the other hand, they may become involved with each other as friends, and continue the relationship after the baby is born. For some girls it may be gratifying to maintain contact with the child through the adopting family, even though the child acknowledges someone else as his mother. But for other girls the situation becomes intolerable. A girl begins to feel jealous of the adoptive mother (which is natural), or she disapproves of the way "her" child is being handled. Or perhaps the adopting family begins to feel threatened whenever the natural mother is around. Conflicts often develop, and of course the child suffers as he wonders to whom he really belongs. One can argue that it would be better to let go of him and place him with total strangers than to risk putting him in the middle of a family tug-of-war. The principal reason why agencies do not identify their clients to one another is to avoid this kind of turmoil.

The Baby Black Market

Although it is unlikely that you will stumble into an *illegal* arrangement, there are two ways you can tell if the proceedings are not legitimate. According to the law, no one is supposed to profit from an adoption placement. The doctor is paid a reasonable medical fee, and the attorney is paid legal fees for drawing up the adoption papers. These fees are usually paid by the adopting parents. If anyone tries to blackmail you or to bribe you with cash or gifts in order to persuade you to surrender your baby, you have good reason to question the legality of the transaction. If anyone allows you to sign final adoption papers *before* your baby is born, you also have grounds for suspicion. If you find yourself in such a situation call the local Legal Aid Society for advice.

Availability of Adoptive Homes

Most girls assume that if they decide to relinquish their babies for adoption there will be no problem finding homes for them. This is not necessarily true. The adoption picture has been changing dramatically in the past twenty years, and permanent homes are not always available to the large number of babies awaiting placement. This is partly because of the medical advances in problems of infertility. Many couples

who would have been unable to produce their own children
previously are now able to do so, and naturally there is no
need for them to consider adopting a child.

In the meantime, many girls who become pregnant are
not as inclined to rush into marriage as they might have been
a few years ago. Now they are much more aware of the consequences of a forced or unhappy marriage. Also, more and
more girls have goals they want to accomplish before they
settle down to rear a family. Consequently, more and more
babies are available for placement in adoptive homes. One
can speculate that the balance may continue to shift depending upon developments in contraceptive devices and
the effect of recent changes in abortion legislation.

WHY PEOPLE ADOPT

The desire for children is fairly strong in most of us, although
having a child means different things to different people.
Ideally a child is wanted for himself and for the delight his
parents can take in nourishing him and watching him grow.
Unfortunately, many people who are not so idealistic take
childbearing for granted as a natural process in the life cycle,
and babies are accepted as the natural by-product of marriage,
regardless of whether or not they are wanted for themselves.

For a woman, having a baby can be the ultimate proof of
her femininity. In becoming a mother, perhaps she acquires a
sense of meaning and purpose that otherwise may have been
lacking in her life. Or a woman's life may already be rich and
full, but all the more so because she has children with whom
to share.

For a man the child is ultimate proof of his virility.
Marrying and having a family suggests that he more or less
believes in the system and that he has a stake in continuing it.
When a married couple has a child, it is proof that they are

both whole and adequate, and everybody is reassured and nods approvingly.

Some couples definitely decide that they do not want children. But what about the couples who do want children and discover that for one reason or another they cannot have any? Such verdicts are usually reached after several years of wishing, hoping, and trying, numerous doctor appointments, and perhaps a sequence of miscarriages. Sometimes it is the man, and sometimes it is the woman, and sometimes it is the combination that does not work. Some couples are advised not to have babies because they will pass on hereditary diseases such as hemophilia. Whatever the causes for not bearing their own children, to some people acquiring a child can become desperately important.

Some couples adopt because they cannot have their own children. Some succeed in having one or two, but are unable to have more, and yet they want a larger family. Others are able to have all the babies they want, but they save room for a few extras, knowing how difficult it is to find homes for babies who have special problems or who are of mixed backgrounds. Whoever the people are who seek to adopt, their reasons for wanting children can be no better or worse than those of most people. But who decides whether or not these people shall have a child, and what are their chances for getting one?

ADOPTION STANDARDS

Because there used to be so many childless couples who wanted to adopt babies, standards were established for selecting the best parents. Like maternity homes, many of the agencies which handle adoption were and continue to be affiliated and sponsored by religious groups. Consequently many of these agencies hold church attendance and religious involvement high on the list of priorities in selecting a couple.

Some of these agencies place babies only in families of one particular faith. If there are no other agencies in the area, this, of course, makes it impossible for a couple of a different faith to adopt unless they are able to find a baby through a doctor or a lawyer.

Other agency policies require that the couple prove that they cannot have children of their own. Some agencies allow only one baby to a family. Often couples have to be within a certain age range or live within a certain geographic area in order to be eligible to adopt a child. Many agencies, instead of relaxing some of the rigid and outdated standards, continue to reject many who would probably make excellent parents. At the same time they turn away many girls who are desperate to find families for their babies.

Some states or counties may have an abundance of babies but a shortage of families seeking adoption. Or the situation may be reversed. Many states have regulations prohibiting any kind of exchange of families or babies across county or state lines, which again prevents many girls from finding sound, permanent placements for their babies. Some agencies are administered by the State Department of Social Welfare. Many girls are reluctant to apply for adoption services there because they do not like the association with Welfare. They assume that if they apply for adoption service at the Welfare department their babies will be placed with people who are poor and uneducated. This is by no means true. If you were interested in adopting a baby, regardless of your income, as you made inquiries about where to apply you would quickly find the Welfare department a central resource for babies of all backgrounds.

The State Departments of Social Welfare and other non-sectarian agencies hire social workers who have at least some professional training in the field of adoption. Consequently in selecting adopting parents these social workers are concerned with factors which will promote the child's physical and emotional growth. Unfortunately the screening process is all too often a social worker's quest for unresolved, unconscious needs in one or both of the marriage partners instead of an effort to help them think together about what makes a healthy and happy environment for a child. Many people find the interviews offensive because of the questions they are asked regarding their marriage, their sexual relationship, family relationships, and other personal aspects of their lives. Some people are defensive because they do in fact have problems in these areas. Others are not accustomed to sharing such matters with total strangers. However, most couples, if they want a baby badly enough, realize that they have no choice but to answer the questions as fully and honestly as they can, no matter how embarrassed and self-conscious they may feel. Many of those who are either turned away by an agency or who find the agency approach too probing, seek babies through independent sources.

By now you can begin to see how complicated the adoption situation is. As you contemplate the placement of your child, you might give some thought to what *you* consider to be a good family. Many girls settle for "a good Christian family" or a family that will be able to afford to send the child to college. But what are the specific aspects of family life that you value and which you would like for your child? This is something to think about and to discuss with your social worker, or your doctor, or with the parents themselves. Most families who adopt can support the child. Of course that is important, but what are people referring to, in addition to economic stability, when they assure you that your baby will be placed in a "good home"? How does this particular agency or social worker or doctor define a good family? If you are not satisfied with what you find out, perhaps you can consult other people involved in adoptions before you make a final decision.

HARD-TO-PLACE BABIES

Even though many babies are happily accepted into adoptive homes every year, it is very difficult to find permanent families for a substantial number of them. Some of these babies are defective at birth, or they are handicapped and may require intensive care. Naturally most people prefer to adopt healthy babies who have the potential to enjoy normal lives. Some of the sick babies are placed in state institutions where they may or may not receive adequate care. Others are placed in special foster homes which are equipped to take care of children with particular kinds of afflictions.

Older children are often hard to place. There may be several children together, brothers and sisters, who have been orphaned or abandoned by their parents. Many of these children have had somewhat traumatic backgrounds. If their sense of trust has been violated, it takes an unusually patient and sensitive family to convince them that they are lovable and wanted. Often these older children wind up in foster homes, which simply reinforces their feeling that nobody wants them.

Another group of children who are especially hard to place are babies who come from mixed racial backgrounds or whose parents belong to a minority group. Traditionally people try to adopt babies who look enough like themselves so that the child can at least appear to be related by blood. Major physical differences between the parents and their child are constant reminders that the child does not "belong." Consequently white people are generally discouraged from adopting babies with Negroid, Oriental, or otherwise "questionable" features. Minority group families do not usually adopt babies of any kind, partly because they cannot afford to. And so these children too grow up unadopted.

Although adoption is unusual in the black community,

some black girls decide to relinquish their babies. These are usually older girls who live away from home. Many white girls give birth to black babies, and may be especially desperate to relinquish them so that their families will never know about their relationship with a black man.

Because of the large number of beautiful, healthy minority babies who are available for adoption, efforts have been made to recruit adoptive parents from minority groups. However, couples with the best intentions often become discouraged by white agency practices which even discourage many white people from following through on adoption applications. Some agencies are beginning to alter their procedures so that some minority-group applicants are approved and at least a few of these babies can be permanently placed. By now a few black babies and various combinations of racially mixed babies have been adopted by white families, and some non-Negro babies have been adopted by black families. Such arrangements, however, are against the law in some Southern states.

Recently we have been hearing more and more about single-parent placements. Many people object to the idea for the same reason they feel that a single mother should give up her baby, but these people fail to realize that two parents are not necessarily available for every child. One loving and devoted parent is certainly better than *no* parent at all.

The Adoption Resource Exchange of North America has been established to improve adoption practices for the benefit of everyone involved. As a central resource which operates on a nationwide basis, it has begun to coordinate the supply of babies on the one hand with the demand for them on the other. The Exchange is especially concerned with placing babies who have special needs and who may therefore require parents who are willing to take on more than the ordinary responsibilities involved in rearing a child. As long as large numbers of people wish to adopt, it is inexcusable for babies and children to grow up in foster care instead of in permanent homes where they can feel that they belong to somebody.

Foster Care

The subject of foster care has come up several times in different contexts. A foster family accepts children on a temporary basis, as compared with an adopting family who accepts a child on a permanent basis. Some foster families take only infants. Others take only children of special ages. Some foster families consist of a mother and a father and perhaps several children. Others are older women, grandmothers or widows, who enjoy having a child or two to look after.

When a family *adopts* a child, they take over the full responsibility for that child. The child assumes the family name, and he becomes heir to the family fortune, if there is one. However, when a child is placed in foster care, he is more like a visitor in someone else's home. Naturally he keeps his own name, and money is paid to the family to cover the cost of clothes and room and board. Sometimes the child's parents pay for his care, but if they cannot afford the full amount, the state pays the balance to the foster family. Some foster families take children because they enjoy them. The more the merrier! But others are fond of the money, and in selecting a foster home it is not always easy to determine the prevailing motive.

During and right after the Second World War, specialists in child development began to realize that orphanages are not especially good places for children. They observed that even though certain institutions were immaculately clean and plenty of good food was available, some of the children failed to develop and some of them actually died. The missing ingredient seemed to be the presence of a warm, mothering person to pick up each baby and hold him and love him and make him feel welcome in the world. Physical care alone was not enough.

Needless to say, these studies startled a number of people. Although orphanages continue to exist, the concept of foster families has been developed and expanded. It was thought that if babies and children could be distributed into small family groups, they would be more likely to receive the individual mothering and attention that is now accepted as absolutely necessary for a child's growth and well-being. In practice, sometimes the children get it, and sometimes they do not.

There are many *good* uses of foster care. For example, a girl might put her baby in foster care while she looks for an apartment and a job; she has no intention of leaving her baby there for any longer than she has to, perhaps for a month at the most. Or after an especially rough delivery a girl might have her child placed in foster care until she is strong enough to take care of the child herself.

On the other hand, foster care can also be misused. Some girls, when they are unable to make a decision about whether to keep or to relinquish their babies, seek foster care as a solution to the dilemma. It is a solution only if there is a very *good* reason for postponing the decision. Otherwise, foster care makes it possible for a mother to go on indefinitely without making a decision, which eventually becomes destructive to the child.

As long as a child is in foster care he still *legally* belongs to his mother, even if she is 3,000 miles away and has not been seen or heard from for a year. Unless she signs papers releasing the child from her legal hold he is not free to be adopted by anyone.

In the meantime, foster parents are supposed to avoid becoming so involved with the child that they will not be able to give him up. The foster mother may be warm and nurturing toward the child; but, knowing that the mother may come at any time and take him away or that he may be transferred to another home, she must not allow herself to love him as if he were her own. The child senses this and begins to develop a basic sense of insecurity. If he is moved from home to home, he feels even more insecure, and eventually he may show signs of a personality disturbance. It becomes increasingly difficult, if not impossible, to repair this kind of damage.

Most mothers who select foster care as an alternative to making long-range plans for their babies are unaware of the unfortunate consequences that may result. Others fail to realize that a baby is not a toy. Just because a baby cannot talk does not mean that he cannot sense and know things. Even though he may seem small and helpless, each day of his life is important as he begins to form an impression of the world, whether it is a good place or a bad place, whether it is a safe place or a scary place. This also applies to his impressions of people, whether they are dependable and loving or unreliable and indifferent.

Probably the most critical thing in a child's life is to feel loved and *wanted*. A child knows instinctively, without being told, when he is unwanted, and if this is the case he will probably feel unworthy and insecure throughout his lifetime. It is a big responsibility to bring a baby into the world. If you do not sincerely and enthusiastically *want* your baby, then it is honest and responsible to give him to people who have demonstrated that they do want a baby. If you do want your baby and you decide to keep him, it follows that you will give him the love and the comfort and care that characterize responsible parenthood.

CHAPTER FOURTEEN

Counseling and therapy

The term "counseling" is misleading. Technically it means "giving advice," and if a baby is involved it sounds as if whoever proposes to counsel takes it upon himself *to advise* a girl about what to do with her baby. Ideally, counseling or therapy should be directed at clarifying how *you* feel and what *you* want. A good counselor or therapist will help you to know from within yourself what is best for you. He should never take it upon himself to make a decision for you, although you may find that some will try.

PREGNANCY COUNSELING

Different levels of counseling from different sources are available to single pregnant girls depending upon the individual and her situation. First of all there is what we might call "pregnancy counseling," which usually takes place in person, but is occasionally offered over the phone. The purpose of these sessions, which may or may not include the baby's father or members of the girl's family, is to familiarize a pregnant girl with what alternatives she has and to help her make appropriate arrangements according to her decision. People who are in a position to offer such counseling include doctors, social workers, ministers, school counselors, and staff members of Planned Parenthood. For a more complete list, refer back to the chapter on community resources. Hopefully, one way or another, you will be able to find someone to help you decide what you want to do. This may take only a few minutes, or it may take several interviews.

Pregnancy counseling may include making a *tentative* decision about the baby so that an adoption referral can be made if it is appropriate. But remember that no *final* decision can be made about the baby until after he is born.

Pregnancy counseling revolves around very practical questions, such as whether or not you want an abortion. If not, can you stay or will you leave town? Where are you going to live? And how are you going to support yourself? These are concrete problems that have to be solved. Once you appear to be settled, a counselor may say, "You know where to find me if you have any further *problems*." You may want to come back, just to talk, but since you cannot define any special problems, you take the counselor at her word and stay away when actually you are terribly lonely and need desperately to talk to somebody. Well, loneliness is a problem.

SUPPORTIVE COUNSELING

If you do feel kind of lost and alone, you might want to consider regular counseling or therapy sessions in which someone gives you the opportunity to express your thoughts and feelings and perhaps asks questions or makes suggestions when they seem appropriate. The biggest problem in your life may be the pregnancy and making a decision about the baby. If this is the case, counseling interviews will probably focus on feelings related to that. (This will be discussed in more detail a little further on.) On the other hand, you may have more or less resolved your feelings about the pregnancy but find yourself concerned about problems in your family, your relationship with your boyfriend, or what you want to do with your life.

Girls occasionally express the fear that they are crazy. In therapy they talk about their families and the things they have been taught as children and as young adults. The therapist may point out the many contradictions in what they have been taught, and they begin to understand why they have felt confused. They are reassured to discover that they are normal and healthy in many ways, but have had no way of knowing this because everything has been so bizarre around them.

Sometimes girls become terribly unhappy, perhaps at home, or at school or at work. Not knowing what to do about it, they manage to become pregnant so that finally *something* has to change. In other words, sometimes a pregnancy can be a rather desperate cry for HELP! If you suspect that this applies to you, a counselor may be able to help you to understand what was causing you to be unhappy and what you can do to change yourself or your situation.

Counseling can serve many functions. Some girls have never had the opportunity to talk seriously to an adult before. Perhaps through the experience of the pregnancy they become aware for the first time that there is a whole big world full of people and problems that go far beyond the everyday concerns of a single, pregnant girl.

Some girls want the pregnancy to pass as fast as possible, and afterwards they will pretend that it never happened. If a girl denies the pregnancy entirely, there is a good chance that she will feel utterly lost and empty after the baby is born. In most cases it is fairly easy to convince these girls that pregnancy, regardless of the circumstances, is a natural part of life. Some experiences are happy ones. Others are painful and disappointing. But each experience is part of the grit and substance of life, which is what makes it interesting. Sometimes, if nothing else, the pregnancy gives a girl the opportunity to stop and look at where she has been and where she is going.

Counseling interviews will vary according to what is important to each girl. As the pregnancy advances, some girls grow increasingly afraid of delivery. With a counselor you can discuss these fears, and possibly how they relate to earlier hospital experiences. No experience is quite so traumatic if you have someone to anticipate it and share it with.

If the person who helped you with pregnancy counseling is not in an appropriate position to offer further counseling, you might want to find someone else. People who are trained to do counseling will be described further on in this chapter.

FAMILY THERAPY

Another kind of counseling focuses on a girl's relationships with other people. Most often these relationships involve members of her family and sometimes the baby's father. Many agencies encourage the whole family to participate in the counseling experience, possibly individually as well as in a group. The theory is that if everyone has a chance to air his feelings about the pregnancy in front of everyone else, the members of the family will know and trust each other a little more, instead of feeling that they always have to hide their troubles. A few agencies have succeeded in including the baby's father and his family in these sessions.

GROUP DISCUSSIONS; GROUP THERAPY

Group therapy is becoming more and more popular and available. For many, joining a group may seem quite frightening, but it is amazing how friendly and supportive the group members usually are, especially to a newcomer.

In some groups the members sit around in a circle and

discuss their problems. Often it is true that many heads are better than one. Also it can be reassuring to learn that other people have problems similar to yours. Sometimes you can help someone by sharing a solution that has worked well for you.

More and more groups are being started for "unmarried mothers" and their families. Group meetings may be held in maternity homes, at clinics, at the YWCA, and at some Planned Parenthood agencies. Groups for the parents of single, pregnant girls are still rare but can be extremely productive. Some agencies offer group meetings for babies' fathers with male social workers. These too can be interesting and rewarding.

Other groups are more dynamic in nature. These groups consist of a mixture of people, men and women, with all kinds of different problems. As group members begin to interact with one another, patterns are observed and translated in terms of the problems an individual may be having in his personal relationships outside the group. For example, a husband who complains about his marriage may try to dominate the group in much the same way he dominates his family at home. As this is brought to his attention in the group, he can make a choice about whether or not he wants to change. The focus in these groups is very much on the here and now. Groups such as these can be found in clinics and family agencies.

USING COUNSELING TO HELP DECIDE ABOUT THE BABY

Many girls, the moment they realize they are pregnant, decide unequivocally that they will give their babies up for adoption. A few decide with comparable certainty that they will keep their babies. Many of the girls who may have been sure at the beginning change their minds, perhaps once, perhaps as many as a dozen times.

Undergoing a nine-month pregnancy and deciding what to do with the baby is often a complicated process, and it can be helpful and reassuring to have a professional person to talk to as you try to decide what is best for you and your baby. You are bound to experience many mixed emotions. A professional person can help you to recognize and express some of these feelings. As long as you keep them buried inside of you, you are likely to feel anxious and uncomfortable; but if you can allow them to come to the surface, you can see them for what they are, and they will not trouble you as much.

If you have already decided that you want to give your baby up, you may feel threatened if you allow yourself to experience warm and tender feelings toward him. A professional person might ask, "Why shouldn't you love him as most mothers love their babies?" Usually the fear is that if you love him you will not be able to let go of him. This is not necessarily true.

On the other hand, you may find that you love the baby and resent him at the same time for the trouble and discomfort he has caused you. There is no such thing as a *good* or *bad* feeling. Whatever your feelings are, they are a legitimate part of you. How you allow them to influence you is something else.

Through counseling some girls begin to see that their reasons for wanting to keep the baby are tied in with complicated and unresolved feelings toward the baby's father. Once they realize that they do not necessarily want the baby for himself, they are able to make a more honest decision about whether to keep or relinquish him.

Many girls assume that they have to give up their babies because a child has a better chance in life with two parents who already have a home and a steady income. A professional person can help a girl to examine this notion so that she can decide for herself whether it necessarily applies in her situation.

Some girls want to keep their babies, but they are not sure if they can handle all of the responsibilities involved. A counselor can help these girls to evaluate their capabilities. He or she can also help a girl approach her family and various agencies in the community to find out what specific kinds of help may be available once the baby is born.

Sometimes if a girl is very positive about her decision, a counselor may suggest that she consider the opposite alternative. Often the girl interprets this to mean that the counselor thinks she *ought* to give the baby up when she has already made it clear that she has decided to keep him, or vice versa. Actually, the counselor is testing the girl in her decision. Also she is giving her the opportunity to consider both sides while there is still time to weigh the situation objectively. If a girl can articulate to someone else how she has arrived at a particular decision, she will be able to explain it to herself during moments of stress or grave doubt.

If the girl is under great pressure from her family or the baby's father to make a particular decision, a responsible counselor can help her to separate her own feelings and opinions from the influence imposed by others. Even the counselor may have a strong opinion about whether a particular girl can handle the responsibility of a baby; but the decision can only be made by the girl herself. This is important because, in the long run, she will have her own way. If, for example, a girl is pressured into keeping her baby, she can resist by neglecting the baby or abandoning him altogether. If, on the other hand, she is forced to relinquish the baby, she may very well have another one in the near future.

If during your pregnancy and in the weeks immediately following delivery you explore all of the pros and cons of keeping and relinquishing your baby, when you do make a decision you will have the satisfaction of knowing that you made the best possible decision for you and the baby *at this particular time in your life*. Knowing this you are much less likely to be haunted by remorse and regret in the years to come.

Sometimes circumstances make it impossible for a girl to have a legitimate choice. Black girls, for example, are often turned away from agencies, or they are given no guarantee that their babies will be placed in permanent homes. A girl finds it especially difficult to relinquish her baby unless she is assured that the baby will be placed quickly and permanently. Consequently many girls who would prefer to relinquish are compelled to keep their babies and do the best they can.

On the other hand, girls can be coerced into relinquishing their babies because of the prevailing opinion (of professionals as well as family) that this is the best decision for everyone involved. If you find yourself in a situation that conflicts with what you feel, hopefully this book will give you the courage and support to speak out. If you find that the people immediately around you fail to hear, write or call anybody you can think of who might be able to help you exercise your right to choose.

COUNSELORS AND THERAPISTS
One hears a lot about psychotherapy, group therapy, psychoanalysis, and psychiatry. Some people still think these words refer to treatment for people with severe emotional disturbances; this is not necessarily true. Life is much more complicated than it used to be, and many of the simple principles that we used to live by no longer seem to apply. So people go to therapists or counselors for help in sorting things out.

Sometimes the problems are specific. A young man does not know if he should go to a liberal arts college or to a trade school. A young woman wants to move away from home but her parents will not let her. In other instances it is difficult to say exactly what the problem is. A couple finds that their marriage is falling apart. A man is fired from every job after three months. A college student finds himself falling asleep the minute he settles down in the library to study. Many of these people are not sick. But many of them may be unhappy. Sometimes it can be helpful to talk with a person who is trained in counseling or psychotherapy.

Some therapists or counselors have very little training, but they are perceptive and they care enough about the people they are working with to be very helpful. Others have all kinds of professional degrees and years of experience, but their professional aloofness or detachment in a time of crisis is not always especially appropriate or helpful. In choosing a counselor or a therapist, do not put your faith entirely in his title. Pay attention to what he says (and to what he does not say) and to his manner. Make sure that you feel you can trust him. Naturally if you do not trust him you will not feel free to tell him what is on your mind.

Social Workers

You are likely to meet more social workers than any other counselors. (Social workers may also be referred to as "caseworkers.") Social work started out as a profession to help people who were poor or underprivileged in some way. Many social workers are taught to think in terms of the environment in which certain problems occur. If they can precipitate changes in a person's environment, for example by increasing his income or by helping him to find a job, they have contributed to the solution of at least some of his problems. In working with their clients social workers are more inclined than other therapists to make phone calls, home visits, and various referrals.

The formal training of social workers varies, according to the requirements of the various departments and agencies in which they work. Some social workers have completed only one or two years of college. Others have a Master's Degree in Social Work (referred to as an M.S.W.) which involves a bachelor's degree and two additional years of full-time study. Even though there are many specialties and levels of training within the field, everyone is referred to as a social worker, and an outsider can never be sure who has the training and experience to do what.

Most social workers in the *Welfare department* have had at least one or two years of college. In some counties the social workers are required to have four-year college degrees. Their job is to determine whether or not a client and her family are eligible to receive Welfare. Some agencies are beginning to turn this work over to clerks, so that the social workers have more time to spend with their clients on other kinds of problems.

Social workers in the *adoption division* of an agency usually have more training. Many of them are required to have their M.S.W.'s.

People with a variety of backgrounds are employed as social workers in a *maternity home*. The executive director of the home is usually an experienced social worker with a master's degree. If individual counseling is offered at the home the counselor usually has an M.S.W. with special training in psychiatric social work. Many nuns and officers in the Salvation Army have social work training.

You might run into several kinds of social workers in and around a *hospital*. One kind, similar to a Welfare worker and having no advanced training, helps patients figure out how much their bills are and how they are going to pay them. Another kind of social worker, called a medical social worker, who is usually required to have the M.S.W., offers counseling to patients who have various illnesses or are victims of accidents and who may need help in anticipating a totally new life-style. They may also offer counseling and support to the families of patients. Medical social workers help people to find places to stay and to make other kinds of plans for when they leave the hospital. Since having a baby is not exactly an illness, you will probably not be referred to a medical social worker for counseling.

Many hospitals have psychiatric social workers on their staffs. Psychiatric social workers have their master's degrees, and are trained specifically in counseling. Some are part of the general hospital clinic staff. Others are affiliated with the *psychiatric clinic*. If you are receiving medical care at a clinic and would like to talk to someone, ask where you can make an appointment with a psychiatric social worker.

Another place where you can usually find professionally trained social workers is in *family service agencies*, such as Jewish Family Service, Lutheran Family Service, and Catholic Family Service. You do not necessarily have to be a member of the particular faith to qualify for counseling services.

Some social workers who go into *private practice* see a few select patients or clients in their own offices. They are listed under "Social Workers" in the Yellow Pages of the telephone book.

School systems often employ social workers with advanced training in education for a variety of purposes. Social workers on the counseling staffs at *colleges and universities* are usually psychiatric social workers.

Psychologists

Psychology is essentially the study of the mind and mental processes. Psychologists who concern themselves with counseling are called clinical psychologists. Very few professional psychologists have only their bachelor's degree. Some have their master's, but most psychologists today have their doctor's degree, which you can verify by the initials "Ph.D." after their names. (A medical doctor is recognized by the familiar "M.D.") Since a psychologist is *not* a medical doctor, he cannot prescribe medication and he cannot authorize abortions.

Nowadays it takes about two years to complete a master's degree in psychology and from four to seven years to complete a Ph.D. In the course of their training, clinical psychologists study methods for measuring human intelligence, motor skills, aptitudes, and other behaviors. Some of the more familiar testing materials include blocks, pencil and paper tests, ink blots, and number games.

Some maternity homes retain a psychologist on the staff for testing purposes and to offer counseling if and when it is indicated. Psychologists are also found on the psychiatric staffs at clinics and hospitals. Some go into private practice, and are listed under "Psychologists" in the Yellow Pages of the telephone book.

Psychiatrists

A psychiatrist has completed four years of college, four years of medical school, and approximately six additional years of study in the diagnosis and treatment of mental disorders. One usually thinks of a psychiatrist as a man, but many women have been trained in the field. Psychiatry is based on the medical model, which focuses on the study of disease. This is why psychiatrists are associated with mental illness instead of mental health.

When you think about it, some disorders are very great, while others are very small. Just as you do not have to be dying to go to a regular doctor, you do not have to be insane to go to a psychiatrist. Psychiatrists can be very helpful to anyone in distress.

Some maternity homes retain a psychiatrist on the staff to offer counseling to girls with special problems. Psychiatrists are also available through hospitals and clinics. Those in private practice are listed under "Physicians and Surgeons, M.D." in the Yellow Pages of your telephone book.

Psychoanalysts

Psychoanalysts are usually psychiatrists who have even more years of training. Anyone who decides to undergo psychoanalysis usually commits himself to at least four years of treatment. Doctor and patient meet for fifty-minute sessions as often as four or five times a week. It is awkward to begin an analysis in the midst of a pregnancy. Most psychoanalysts would advise you to come back after the baby is born. If you need help immediately, they might refer you to a counselor who offers less intensive therapy.

Nurses

There is an increasing number of nurses who are receiving training in counseling. Some are trained as psychiatric nurses. Others are trained in specific areas of public health. You may find a nurse extremely helpful as someone to talk to before delivery, while you are in the hospital, or later on when you are concerned about problems with child care.

COST OF COUNSELING

An adoption agency does not charge for its counseling service to natural mothers.

If you receive counseling as a resident in a maternity home, the cost will be included in your total fee as arranged at the time of admission. If you are referred to the staff psychiatrist, there *may* be an additional charge depending upon the arrangement the home has with the doctor.

Many hospitals and clinics scale their fees according to

the individual's ability to pay. (For more information regarding scaled fees, see page 74.) One counseling interview may cost you nothing. On the other hand, you may be charged anywhere from $1 to $30, depending on the policy of the clinic. The same applies to family service agencies. Sometimes the cost of counseling interviews is covered by Medicaid. This is worth investigating.

Social workers in private practice charge around $15 per interview. Psychologists charge $20 to $30. Psychiatrists charge from $25 to $50. Prices vary in different parts of the United States and according to the reputation of the therapist.

The cost of group therapy varies according to where and how often the group meets. Sessions usually last at least an hour and a half and often considerably longer. The cost may vary from $5 to $15 per session, or it may be scaled according to the individual's ability to pay.

Fees can be a problem. You may need or want counseling very badly, but, considering your finances, it seems outrageous to pay $15 just to *talk* to somebody. If low-cost counseling is not available through a clinic or agency, you may be able to find a therapist who will make a special arrangement with you. Money, like everything else, is a legitimate *problem* to bring up with a counselor or therapist.

* * *

Counseling and psychotherapy can be helpful to many girls who would not necessarily think to pursue it on their own. An unexpected pregnancy in the life of a single woman can bring to the surface all kinds of problems that she has never had to deal with before. Competent professional help may enable her to confront her difficulties (and herself) for the first time, and to experience the pregnancy as the beginning of a more rich and meaningful life.

CHAPTER FIFTEEN

Hospitalization and delivery

Many hospitals offer a regularly scheduled tour for their pregnant patients so that when they come in to have their babies everything will not appear so strange and possibly frightening to them. If you have a chance to take such a tour, it is strongly recommended.

As the time nears for you to deliver, your doctor will tell you what signs to watch out for. You will know to call him or the hospital immediately if your water bag breaks, if you have what is called a "bloody show," or if you experience painful contractions. He will teach you to time your contractions, and he will tell you at what stage to come into the hospital. It is a good idea to have the phone number and the address of the hospital available at all times. If you are familiar with the hospital, you will know exactly where to go and what to do when you get there.

Some women go to the hospital by themselves. Others are accompanied by a friend or their parents. This may also be true of married women since husbands are not always available for the traditional smoking and pacing. Some hospitals permit one visitor in the labor room with the patient. It can be reassuring to have somebody there to talk to and to encourage you as you begin to feel things happening.

Labor can be very quick or very long. It is different for

everyone. Sometimes during labor girls finally realize for the first time what these last nine months have been all about.

Before delivery, some girls request anesthesia in order to sleep through the entire experience. Anesthesia may be used eventually, but doctors are reluctant to put a patient completely to sleep, partly because they need her participation in the delivery process. Babies do not exactly fall out. They need a push. In addition, anesthetics that are powerful enough to put the mother to sleep may harm the baby.

Delivery itself is an awesome event. It may be very quick and simple, or it can become quite complicated. If you are curious about what is going on, do not be afraid to ask. Some girls feel that because everybody knows they are single and giving the baby up they have no right to complain about the pain or to participate in what is happening.

Unless a mother plans to keep and nurse her baby she will be given a shot immediately after delivery to dry up her milk.

THE "OLD" APPROACH

Hospitals have different policies regarding their single maternity patients. The old-fashioned approach is inspired by the attitude that most girls should give up their babies for adoption. If you definitely plan to keep your baby, you *may* be treated as any other patient on the maternity ward, and in that case, much of what follows may not apply to you. On the other hand, if you definitely plan to relinquish your child, or if it is indicated in your record that you are still undecided, you might consider what follows in selecting the hospital where you plan to give birth.

For years it has been thought that if a girl has contact with her baby, her strong maternal feelings will make it impossible for her to part with the child. Consequently, many hospitals and maternity homes have devised a routine that theoretically protects girls from this terrible conflict. According to the old approach, the mirrors are turned to the wall so that the girl cannot watch the delivery. The baby is rushed immediately out of the delivery room so that the mother will be spared the anguish of either seeing her child or hearing him cry. Some girls never even know if they had a boy or a girl.

Following delivery the girls are placed on a separate wing or floor from the maternity ward so that they will not be in contact with the other mothers and their babies. Sometimes girls are allowed to view their babies once or twice but they are discouraged from lingering near the nursery window. Sometimes they see the baby once when the adoption worker comes to take him from the hospital.

THE "NEW" APPROACH

Many hospitals and maternity homes have evolved a more modern attitude toward the relationship between a single mother and her child. It is felt that any woman after carrying the baby for so many months and after feeling him grow and develop into a little character with all kinds of strange habits, will naturally want to see him and touch him and hold him after he is born.

During pregnancy most women worry about whether or not the baby will be healthy and whole when he is born. Invariably a mother is reassured when finally she can take all the blankets and wrappings away and study the baby from head to foot. She counts his fingers and his toes, and she examines his umbilicus. She determines for herself that the baby is wonderful and fine. And she wants to see what he looks like. Does he resemble her or his father?

Girls who give their babies up for adoption without ever seeing or examining them often have a recurring fear that perhaps their babies were defective but no one told them. When they marry and become pregnant for a second time, instead of developing the warm, tender feelings that mothers usually have toward their babies, many of these girls feel aloof and detached. In the first pregnancy the natural mothering process was interrupted abruptly at the moment of delivery. Now even though the girl is married and knows intellectually that she will be keeping this baby, emotionally she prepares herself to experience loss and separation.

Some hospitals and maternity homes feel that the old approach, which discourages a girl from having anything to do with her baby, is somewhat inhumane and unrealistic. Consequently, the staff and social workers encourage a girl at least to see her baby. Girls who are familiar with the old approach are usually enormously relieved to know that they will be able to see (and feed) their babies if they want to. Of course it is difficult to give up a baby you have seen and fed and loved, but at least the baby is a real baby, and not a fantasy baby whom you carried but never knew.

MATERNITY WARDS

Hospitals have different policies regarding the amount of contact that is permitted between *any* mother and her child. Traditionally hospitals keep all of the babies in a large nursery where they are bathed and cared for by the staff. Two or three times a day they are wheeled out to the mothers in their rooms to be fed. Some hospitals are so fastidious about germs that they scarcely allow a mother to touch her child. Others recognize the psychological importance of allowing the mother to love and touch her baby in a natural and spontaneous way.

"*Rooming-in*," which is available in some hospitals, permits the child to be in the same room with the mother most of the time. The mother feeds her child and changes and bathes him herself. This is an excellent opportunity for inexperienced mothers to learn child care under the supervision of the staff nurses.

Your Reactions to Your Baby

It is hard to predict how you will feel toward your baby when he arrives. Some girls are suddenly overcome by maternal feelings that they never expected of themselves. Others reluctantly admit that they cannot conjure up any maternal feelings toward the child at all. Some of these girls become more enthusiastic about their babies on the second or third day in the hospital. Some girls who were determined to relinquish their babies change their minds and make arrangements to keep them. Girls who were undecided before delivery may begin to feel the responsibilities involved in keeping a child, and either welcome the challenge or decide to postpone it until some other time in their lives. Strong feelings are invariably evoked by the arrival of twins. Finally, there are the girls who feel that they have to give up the baby, for any number of reasons, but who want so much to keep him. These girls suffer greatly in the weeks that follow.

Contact with Other Patients

Girls who feel compelled to give their babies up may find it especially difficult to be around other mothers who will be taking their babies home. Separating single mothers from the other mothers also spares them from embarrassing questions that are frequently asked by friendly and well-meaning patients: "Is your husband visiting tonight?" "Isn't your baby going home with you?" Presumably you have enough on your mind without having to explain your situation to the stranger in the next bed, and making up a plausible "story" can quickly become tiresome.

Single mothers may be segregated into one or two rooms

on the maternity ward for other reasons. Some girls are afraid of being recognized by other patients or their visitors. Since patients' names are posted on the doors to their rooms, girls often make up names to use in the hospital.

Some hospitals put all of the maternity patients together without any special concern for whether they are married or single. If you have befriended a number of other single, pregnant girls, it may be rather revealing to the other patients if *all* of these friends come to visit you. However, do not worry *too* much about the lady in the next bed. For all you know, she is not married either.

Married women have unpredictable reactions to single mothers. Some are extremely sympathetic. Others are quite insensitive: "How can you *give up* your baby?" Some women become very maternal and involved. Others are indignant. This is especially true of women who have had problems becoming pregnant and carrying a baby to term. To them it appears that the single girl recklessly produces a child whom she gives up with equal abandon. Few people really know or understand what a single girl goes through unless perhaps they have been through it themselves. And even then the experience is different for everyone.

THE STAFF

Most of the people on the staff at the hospital know from your chart what your situation is. They refer to you as "Mrs. So-and-So" as a matter of habit, since most of their patients are married and it would be an effort to remember which ones are "Miss." Usually the staff will go to great lengths to protect you and your privacy. Sometimes they are so good at helping you to keep up a front (whatever it is) that you wonder yourself whether they know or not. If you have any questions or problems, you can always go to the nurses' station and ask to speak to a nurse privately.

While you are in the hospital you are bound to experience a jumble of emotions. This is true for every mother. On the one hand you are elated and relieved that all these months of waiting are finally over. You rejoice at the fine baby you have produced, and you can actually see your toes for the first time in several months. On the other hand, this experience, for whatever it has meant to you, is coming to an end. It is time to go on from here. The past, no matter how painful, is at least familiar, and in that regard it is safe. But the future is invariably uncertain, and suddenly it can appear very frightening.

Some of what you feel will be caused by various changes in your body chemistry. Delivery is a traumatic event! Many women feel wonderful for the first couple of days, then suddenly they begin to feel weepy and depressed. Even though you may have good reasons for feeling unhappy, you may experience feelings even more strongly because of the hormonal changes that are taking place in your body. Do not be frightened by mood shifts while you are in the hospital. Enjoy your happiness and, on the other hand, allow your tears to flow freely. If things begin to get out of-control, find a staff member and tell her your problem. Talking to someone can be helpful.

Pediatricians

Doctors who specialize in the care of infants and children are called pediatricians. As soon as your baby is born, a pediatrician will check him over very carefully, and if he has any questions about the baby's health he will prescribe appropriate tests. Remember that as the baby's mother *you* are responsible for the baby until you sign papers that state otherwise. Do not be surprised if the doctor requests your signature on papers authorizing tests or certain kinds of medication or treatment.

If your child is a boy, the doctor will need your permission before he can perform a circumcision. This is the surgical removal of the foreskin from the end of the baby's penis. This operation, though customary, is generally unnecessary and is completely at the discretion of the mother.

Sometimes doctors scurry about looking busy and important and use words you cannot understand. No matter what happens, do not forget that *you* are the baby's mother and have every right to know what is happening to your child. If you are not satisfied by what the nurses tell you, request a chance to talk to the doctor.

Your Own Medical Condition

Of course you will be tender from your episiotomy. (An episiotomy is the incision which is made immediately before delivery to enlarge the vaginal opening so that the baby can pass through easily.) Some girls feel very sore, especially when they try to walk. Others bounce out of bed the first day, almost as if nothing had happened. It is not unusual for a variety of complications to arise following delivery. Doctors and nurses will keep a close eye on you for signs of infection. Their recommendations for your care and the length of your stay in the hospital will depend upon the details of your delivery and your general state of health.

BIRTH CERTIFICATES

While you are still in the hospital a nurse or secretary will ask you to fill out a birth certificate. If you are keeping your baby, you will want to fill out the birth certificate as accurately as possible, since this will be your child's primary source of identification for the rest of his life. In a few states birth certificates still indicate whether or not a child is legitimate. If you have had contact with an attorney or an adoption worker, you might consult him or her about filling out the birth certificate to the child's best advantage. Otherwise, contact someone in the adoption unit in the State Department of Social Welfare, or call the Registrar at the local Health Department.

One important question is how to fill out the section pertaining to the baby's father. If you leave those lines blank, the father is presumed to be unknown and the child is unmistakably illegitimate to anyone who even glances at the document. On the other hand, if you fill in the correct name, naturally it will not be the same as both yours and the child's. You can make it appear that you are married, but then, if and when you do marry and your husband wants to adopt your child, you have to *prove* that you were not married when you said that you were. Otherwise the man described on the birth certificate as your husband has to be located in order to relinquish his rights as the father of the child.

Birth certificates can be changed, but it is easier for everyone involved if they are filled out appropriately at the beginning. Some states have considered issuing identification cards which would omit information regarding the legitimacy of a child. However, these cards would be pointless unless they were issued to *all* children.

If you plan to relinquish your baby for adoption, what you put on the birth certificate is not so critical. It is nice to give your baby a name so you can refer to him specifically instead of as "the baby." The information that you give about yourself and the baby's father is entirely up to you. Some of the questions are asked simply for statistical purposes. Once the baby has been adopted, a new birth certificate will be issued, and the original will be sealed in a vault. Only in unusual circumstances can anyone refer to it again.

Hospitals usually release a report of births to the local newspapers. Generally they also send a copy of a baby's birth certificate to the mother's home county as a matter of record.

The information may be reported in the local newspapers under the section titled "Birth Record" or "Vital Statistics." When you fill out your baby's birth certificate in the hospital, ask what the policy is and make sure that they are not about to send a copy of the birth certificate somewhere you do not want it to go.

INFANT RELEASE FORMS

There was a time when almost anybody could go into a nursery, pick up a baby, and walk out with him. Naturally it was rather upsetting to the mother when it was discovered that her child had disappeared. Consequently, in many hospitals Infant Release forms must be filled out if *anyone* other than the natural mother is to take the baby away from the hospital. This applies to the baby's father, other relatives, adoption workers, and adopting parents. The natural mother signs her consent to let a specifically named person or persons take the baby from the hospital. The person taking the baby must be able to identify him or herself properly before the child can be released.

It should be reassuring to know that no one can walk off with your baby without your permission. However, girls sometimes confuse Infant Release papers with *relinquishment* papers and suspect they are being tricked into signing *final* papers before they are ready. Remember that all you are doing is authorizing someone other than yourself to take the baby from the hospital.

DISCHARGE FROM THE HOSPITAL

Following a normal delivery, most hospitals recommend that their maternity patients stay for three or four days to rest and recover. (For some women with families, this is the only rest they ever get.)

If you are affiliated with a maternity home, you may be

discharged earlier to the care of the nursing staff at the home. If the home has a nursery, possibly you will take the baby with you from the hospital.

If you are keeping your baby, you will probably have arranged to go directly from the hospital to your home or to an apartment. A few maternity homes have temporary facilities for girls who keep their babies. Some girls place their babies temporarily in foster care until they get organized. (Some of the services that are available to single mothers will be discussed in more detail in the final chapter.)

Before any girl may leave the hospital, she must have *some* plan for her baby. If she is not planning to take the baby from the hospital herself, she must have definite arrangements for someone else to come and pick him up. Otherwise she will be detained in the hospital (possibly at her own expense) until some kind of plan has been formulated.

When a girl decides to relinquish her baby for adoption, the procedures and formalities depend upon the philosophy of the people involved. Sometimes a girl waves good-bye to her baby through the nursery window at the hospital or brings him to the adoption agency or the maternity home where she gives him to the adoption worker. Sometimes she signs the final papers at the same time she says good-bye to him.

It is difficult to say what the best procedure is. Babies are very helpless and engaging little beings, and it is not easy for any girl to give or sign her baby away forever. People can try to be helpful to her, but they cannot spare her whatever pain she feels. Some of the practices in different maternity homes and adoption agencies seem unnecessarily cruel. Nevertheless, most girls somehow seem to be able to do whatever they are expected to do when the time comes. And·they go on, at least for the time being. Some come back. . . .

and your baby may be in excellent health, make sure that you are covered by some kind of health insurance, possibly through your family, through the baby's father, or through your job. In case of emergency there is always the county hospital, but it may be very old and very crowded. If you have no medical or health insurance, call the Welfare department and find out what state Medical Aid program applies to you.

Contraception and Sex Education

Contraception and sex education are absolutely essential to your health and happiness. If you are uncomfortable about talking to your own doctor, seek out one of the Planned Parenthood Centers listed in the back of this book. Or ask the Public Health Department where you can obtain information and supplies. If no doctor or clinic is available to help you in your immediate area, you may have to travel to another city, but it is worth it to avoid becoming pregnant until you are ready to have another baby.

La Leche Groups

La Leche International (*leche* means milk in Spanish) is an organization for mothers who are interested in breastfeeding their babies. Small groups are located in towns and cities all over the United States. Sometimes they are listed under "La Leche" in the white pages of the telephone book; or you may have to write to the national headquarters to find out where the nearest one is located:

La Leche International
9616 Minnesota Avenue
Franklin Park, Illinois 60131
    Telephone: (312) 455-7730

The group meetings are usually informal. Mothers get together to discuss various aspects of breastfeeding and are available to help each other when nursing problems arise. In some cities La Leche runs a mother's milk bank which you may want to inquire about.

Counseling

You may find that working and taking care of the baby are more than you can handle. Or you may feel that you are slowly going out of your head for other reasons. If you are on Welfare, your social worker *may* have some time to talk about these things with you. If she does not, maybe she can suggest someone else for you to see. You may find it helpful to talk to a Public Health Nurse.

Some agencies hold regular group meetings for single mothers who need help with some of their problems. Such agencies include:

Welfare departments
YWCA
Maternity homes
Family service organizations
Hospitals

If you are interested, call any of the above and see if someone knows about a group you can join.

If you prefer to see an individual therapist and you do not want the Welfare department involved in your personal problems, refer back to the chapter on counseling. Your State Bureau of Mental Hygiene may also be able to offer information about counseling and psychotherapy.

Social Life and Recreation

Nothing is worse for the morale than staying inside all day.

Undoubtedly you get plenty of exercise taking care of the baby, but you need other kinds of exercise too. You need variety in your daily life, which may mean joining a bowling team, taking a macramé class, going out for a beer on Friday nights, or swimming at the YWCA. Whatever you do, you must allow yourself at least a little bit of time and a little bit of money to have FUN!

COMMON PROBLEMS

Isolation

The most critical problem that a single mother may have is feeling cut off and isolated from the rest of the world. Once you have a baby, you can no longer go anywhere without either taking the baby with you or finding a sitter. The baby may provide some measure of company, but most of us require adult company as well. Nothing is worse than feeling lonely and unloved and as if nobody in the whole world cares, except maybe the baby.

Sometimes girls find that they lose friends when they keep their babies. This is partly because many single mothers are no longer as available and interested in going out as they used to be. Also, most girls' interests change when they assume the responsibility of caring for a child. Perhaps in the meantime they acquire new friends.

Girls who find themselves cut off and isolated from their families and friends often become discouraged and depressed. There is little joy in their lives to offset the everyday monotony and drudgery. If finances are at a low ebb and the baby is teething and fussy, it is easy to become anxious and impatient. Sometimes mothers find themselves shouting at their babies or struggling with strong impulses to harm them in some way. These moments can be terrifying, especially be-

cause the mother loves her child and she knows how helpless
he is. She begins to wonder if she did the right thing to keep
him, and she begins to feel guilty because she considers herself
inadequate as a mother.

Anybody would feel discouraged in the same situation!
If you begin to feel trapped, get help. If you cannot think of
anyone to consult, go see a minister or a rabbi. Or call Suicide
Prevention for suggestions on what you can do to alter the
situation (see page 50).

Sometimes girls know they need help but they are not
sure what to ask for. If you say, "I am so miserable I don't
know what to do," perhaps the other person can help clarify
what some of the problems are so that you can begin to find
solutions. Or you can say, "I feel trapped," or "I feel lonely."
Most people assume that you are fine unless you *tell* them that
you are hurting, even if you do not know where or why.

How Do You Present Yourself?

Are you "Miss" or "Mrs."? Do you say that you are widowed
or divorced—or single? Do you wear a wedding band?

The answer to all of these questions depends upon how
brave you are and what attitude prevails in the community
where you live. It makes a difference if you have the support
of other single mothers or if you are the only one you know.
There may also be a difference in what you tell casual ac-
quaintances and those who become your close friends.

If you sense that people will feel uncomfortable with the
truth, especially if it may be to your disadvantage, as in a job
situation, it is probably wise to say you are widowed or divorced. Whether or not people believe you is their problem.
The details are none of their business.

Many girls simply change the "Miss" to "Mrs." in front
of their names. This is easier to do when you go to a new
place where you were not previously known as "Miss."

Whether or not you wear a wedding ring also depends upon you and the attitudes around you. Wearing one of course suggests to the world that you are married and may discourage (some) young men from asking you out on a date. If you decide to wear a ring, perhaps the best solution is to wear one on the fourth finger of your right hand as many divorced and widowed women do.

Men

What about men? Many, many single mothers get married, some of them to the baby's father, others to men they met long before the baby was born, during the pregnancy, or afterwards. It does not seem to make a lot of difference. Usually when a relationship becomes serious you can sense if the man can love and accept your child or if he is jealous and threatened by the constant evidence of a previous relationship. This is something you have to work out together.

Girls who keep their babies express concern about rearing their children without fathers. If a girl has an active dating life the hazard is that the child will have *too many* fathers. Any child who grows up with a single parent usually shows a strong need for affection from adults of the opposite sex. You may find your child jumping into the lap of every man who enters your house—and getting a variety of responses from your male guests!

What Do You Tell Your Child?

The answer to this question will depend entirely upon the circumstances. By the time your child wants to know and is old enough to understand about his father, you may be happily married, and it may not be necessary to go into a long, complicated explanation. If you have presented yourself to the rest of the world as widowed or divorced, you may want to offer this explanation to your child as well until he is older and you choose to tell him otherwise.

Some children are infinitely curious about their origins. Others take them for granted. When your child asks about his father, listen to him. Hear him. He will tell you what he wants to know and what he is ready to hear. If a child feels well loved for himself and has been allowed to develop a strong sense of his right-to-be, he will manage.

Appendix

ABORTION REFERRALS

Call the telephone number listed for your own state or the state nearest to you. A recording will give you the names and phone numbers of several clergymen whom you can call to arrange a personal interview to discuss where you can go to receive a safe abortion.

California	(213) 666-7600
Connecticut	(203) 624-8646
Illinois	(312) 667-6015
Iowa	(515) 282-1738
Massachusetts	(617) 527-7188
Michigan	(313) 964-0838
New Jersey	(201) 933-2937
New York	(607) 272-7172
New York City	(212) 477-0034
Ohio	(216) 229-7423
Pennsylvania	(215) WA3-5141

PLANNED PARENTHOOD AFFILIATES

Call the office that is closest to you for information about pregnancy tests, the Morning-After Treatment, birth control information and devices, tests and treatment for venereal diseases, abortion referrals, and referrals for responsible medical care:*

ALABAMA

Birmingham

Planned Parenthood League of Alabama
1714 Eleventh Avenue   (35205)
Tel.: (205) 328-8196

Huntsville

Planned Parenthood Association of Madison County
614 Madison Street, Suite 3   (35801)
Tel.: (205) 534-0211

ALASKA

Anchorage

Anchorage Planned Parenthood League
327 Eagle Street   (99501)
Tel.: (907) 272-1214

ARIZONA

Phoenix

Planned Parenthood Association of Phoenix
1200 South 5th Avenue   (85003)
Tel.: (602) 252-8861

Tucson

Planned Parenthood Center of Tucson, Inc.
127 South Fifth Avenue (85701)
Tel.: (602) 623-0349

* This list was published by the Planned Parenthood Federation of America, Inc. (New York, August 1969).

CALIFORNIA

Bakersfield
    Planned Parenthood Association of Kern County
    238-18th St.   (93301)
    Tel.: (805) 322-0859
Los Angeles
    Planned Parenthood World Population/Los Angeles
    3100 West Eighth Street   (90005)
    Tel.: (213) 380-9300
Oakland
    Planned Parenthood League of Alameda County
    482 West MacArthur Boulevard   (94609)
    Tel.: (415) 654-7987
Pasadena
    Pasadena Planned Parenthood Committee
    1200 North Lake Avenue   (91104)
    Tel.: (213) 794-0513
Sacramento
    Planned Parenthood Association of Sacramento
    922-29th Street   (95816)
    Tel.: (916) 446-5034
San Bernardino
    Planned Parenthood Council of San Bernardino County
    P.O. Box 70   (92401)
    Tel.: (714) 885-0231
San Diego
    Planned Parenthood Association of San Diego County
    1369 B Street   (92101)
    Tel.: (714) 223-7638
San Francisco
    Planned Parenthood Association of San Francisco
    2340 Clay Street   (94115)
    Tel.: (415) 922-1720

San Jose
> Planned Parenthood Association of Santa Clara County
> 28 North 16th Street   (95112)
> Tel.: (408) 294-2442

San Mateo
> Planned Parenthood of San Mateo County
> 35 North "B" Street   (94401)
> Tel.: (415) 344-6864

San Rafael
> Planned Parenthood Association of Marin County
> 603 D Street   (94901)
> Tel.: (415) 454-0471

Santa Ana
> Planned Parenthood Association of Orange County
> 211 South Broadway   (92701)
> Tel.: (714) 541-6233

Santa Barbara
> Planned Parenthood of Santa Barbara
> 226 East de la Guerra Street   (93101)
> Tel.: (815) 963-4417

Walnut Creek
> Planned Parenthood of Contra Costa County
> 1291 Oakland Boulevard   (94596)
> Tel.: (415) 825-0790

COLORADO

Denver
> Planned Parenthood of Colorado
> 2025 York Street   (80205)
> Tel.: (303) 388-4215

CONNECTICUT

New Haven
> Planned Parenthood League of Connecticut

406 Orange Street   (06511)
Tel.: (203) UN 5-0595

DELAWARE

Wilmington
  Delaware League for Planned Parenthood
  800 Washington Street   (19801)
  Tel.: (302) OL 5-8852

DISTRICT OF COLUMBIA

Washington
  Planned Parenthood of Metropolitan Washington, D.C.
  1109 M Street, N.W.   (20005)
  Tel.: (202) DU 7-8787

FLORIDA

Clearwater Beach
  Planned Parenthood Education Committee of Pinellas
    County
  P.O. Box 3005   (33515)
  Tel.: (813) 446-2139
Jacksonville
  Planned Parenthood of Northeast Florida, Inc.
  2255 Phyliss Street, Suite 101   (32204)
  Tel.: (904) 388-3568
Sarasota
  Planned Parenthood Association of Sarasota, Inc.
  P.O. Box 2532   (33578)
  Tel.: (813) 955-8055

GEORGIA

Atlanta
  Planned Parenthood Association of the Atlanta Area
  118 Marietta Street, N.W.   (30303)
  Tel.: (404) 523-6996

Augusta
Augusta Planned Parenthood Association, Inc.
P.O. Box 3293-Hill Station (30904)
Tel.: (404) 724-7111-Ext. 510

Savannah
Planned Parenthood Association of Chatham County
2512 Habersham Street (31401)
Tel.: (912) 236-4207

HAWAII

Honolulu
Hawaii Planned Parenthood Committee
1301 Punch Bowl Street (96813)
Tel.: (808) 562-087

ILLINOIS

Champaign
Planned Parenthood Association of Champaign County
505 South Fifth Street (61801)
Tel.: (217) 352-7961

Chicago
Planned Parenthood Association—Chicago Area
185 North Wabash Avenue (60601)
Tel.: (312) 726-5134

Peoria
Planned Parenthood Association of Peoria Area
410 Fayette, Room 10 (61602)
Tel.: (309) 673-6911

INDIANA

Anderson
Planned Parenthood of Madison County
1407 Locust Street (46011)
Tel.: (317) 649-2281

Bloomington
>   Planned Parenthood Association of Monroe County
>   717 West Fourth Street   (47401)
>   Tel.: (812) 339-2469

Evansville
>   Planned Parenthood of Evansville
>   221 South East 8th Street   (47713)
>   Tel.: (812) 423-6277

Gary
>   Planned Parenthood of Northwestern Indiana, Inc.
>   625 Washington Street   (46402)
>   Tel.: (219) 883-9567

Indianapolis
>   Planned Parenthood Association of Indianapolis
>   Room 108, 615 North Alabama Street   (46204)
>   Tel.: (317) 634-8019

Lafayette
>   Planned Parenthood Association of Tippecanoe County
>   P.O. Box 1114   (47902)
>   Tel.: (317) 743-9418

Muncie
>   Planned Parenthood of Delaware County
>   418 West Adams   (47305)
>   Tel.: (317) 282-8011

South Bend
>   Planned Parenthood of North Central Indiana
>   1419 South Michigan Street   (46613)
>   Tel.: (219) 289-8461

IOWA

Des Moines
>   Planned Parenthood of Iowa
>   851 19th Street   (50314)
>   Tel.: (515) 282-2101

Sioux City
Planned Parenthood Committee of Sioux City
Y.W.C.A.—619 Sixth Street   (51101)
Tel.: (515) 258-4019

KANSAS (*See Kansas City, Mo.*)

KENTUCKY
Berea
The Mountain Maternal Health League
3 Prospect Street   (40403)
Tel.: (606) 986-4677
Lexington
Planned Parenthood of Lexington
868 Georgetown Street   (40505)
Tel.: (606) 255-4913
Louisville
Planned Parenthood Center
725 East Broadway   (40202)
Tel.: (502) 587-6454

MARYLAND
Baltimore
Planned Parenthood Association of Maryland, Inc.
517 North Charles Street   (21201)
Tel.: (301) PL 2-0131
Silver Spring
(See D.C. listing)
Montgomery County, Maryland Branch
344 University Boulevard, West, Suite #325   (20901)
Tel.: (301) 593-0800

MASSACHUSETTS
Boston
Planned Parenthood League of Massachusetts

229 Berkeley Street   (02116)
Tel.: (617) KE 6-8790

MICHIGAN

Ann Arbor
The Washtenaw County League for Planned Parenthood
122½ East Liberty Street   (48103)
Tel.: (313) 663-3306

Detroit
Planned Parenthood League, Inc.
Professional Plaza Concourse Building
3750 Woodward Avenue   (48201)
Tel.: (313) 832-7200

Flint
Flint Community Planned Parenthood Association
1019 Manning Street   (48503)
Tel.: (313) 238-3631

Grand Rapids
Planned Parenthood Association/Kent County
45 Barclay, N.E.   (49502)
Tel.: (616) 459-3101

Kalamazoo
Planned Parenthood Association of Kalamazoo County, Michigan, Inc.
231 East Ransom   (49006)
Tel.: (616) 349-9439

Lansing
Planned Parenthood of Greater Lansing
Box 2241-Michigan Avenue Station   (48911)
Tel.: (517) 355-7926

Monroe
Planned Parenthood of Monroe County
Box 487   (48161)
Tel.: (313) 242-2711

Muskegon
> Muskegon Area Planned Parenthood Association, Inc.
> 1095 Third Street   (49440)
> Tel.: (616) 722-2928

Saginaw
> Planned Parenthood Association of Saginaw, Inc.
> 720 Tuscola Street   (48607)
> Tel.: (517) 755-1144

MINNESOTA

Minneapolis
> Planned Parenthood of Minneapolis
> 223 Walker Building
> 803 Hennepin Avenue   (55403)
> Tel.: (612) 336-8931

St. Paul
> Planned Parenthood of St. Paul
> 408 Hamm Building
> 408 St. Peter Street   (55102)
> Tel.: (612) 224-1361

MISSOURI

Kansas City
> Planned Parenthood Association of Greater
>   Kansas City
> 3222½ Troost Avenue   (64109)
> Tel.: (816) WE 1-4121

St. Louis
> Planned Parenthood Association of St. Louis
> 4947 Delmar Boulevard   (63108)
> Tel.: (314) FO 1-6360

MONTANA

Missoula
> Planned Parenthood of Missoula County

Health Department Courthouse Annex
Tel.: (406) 549-2374

NEBRASKA

Omaha
Planned Parenthood Committee of Nebraska
510 South 41 Street   (68105)
Tel.: (402) 342-2400

NEW HAMPSHIRE

Keene
Planned Parenthood Association of Southwestern
    New Hampshire
305 Main Street   (03431)
Tel.: (603) 352-8616
Lebanon
Planned Parenthood Association of the Upper Valley
14 Parkhurst Street   (03766)
Tel.: (603) 448-1214

NEW JERSEY

Asbury Park
Planned Parenthood of Monmouth County
913 Sewell Avenue   (07712)
Tel.: (201) 774-2550
Camden
Planned Parenthood Greater Camden Area
590 Benson Street   (08103)
Tel.: (609) 365-3519
Hackensack
Planned Parenthood Center of Bergen County
59 Essex Street   (07601)
Tel.: (201) HU 9-1155

Jersey City
Planned Parenthood Association of Hudson County
777 Bergen Avenue, Room 218
Tel.: (201) 332-2565
Morristown
Planned Parenthood Center—Morris Area
10 Pine Street   (07960)
Tel.: (201) JE 9-1364
Newark
Planned Parenthood-Essex County
15 William Street   (07102)
Tel.: (201) 642-0604
Paterson
Passaic County Planned Parenthood Center
105 Presidential Boulevard
Riverview Towers Building #2   (07522)
Tel.: (201) AR 4-4925
Plainfield
Planned Parenthood Tri-County League
234 Park Avenue   (07060)
Tel.: (201) PL 6-3736
Trenton
Planned Parenthood Association of Mercer Area
211 Academy Street   (08618)
Tel.: (609) 599-3736

NEW MEXICO
Albuquerque
Bernalillo County Planned Parenthood Association
1111 Stanford Drive, N.E.   (87106)
Tel.: (505) 268-4535
Las Cruces
Dona Ana County Planned Parenthood Association

221 West Griggs Avenue   (88001)
Tel.: (505) JA 4-1571

NEW YORK

Albany
Planned Parenthood Association of Albany
225 Lark Street   (12210)
Tel.: (518) AL 3-5430

Albion
Planned Parenthood of Orleans County
South Main Street   (14411)

Babylon
Planned Parenthood of South Suffolk
215 Deer Park Avenue   (11702)
Tel.: (516) MO 9-1590

Binghamton
Broome County Planned Parenthood Center
710 O'Neil Bldg.   (13901)
Tel.: (607) 723-8306

Buffalo
Planned Parenthood Center of Buffalo
210 Franklin Street   (14202)
Tel.: (716) 853-1771

Elmira
Planned Parenthood of Chemung County-Corning Inc.
200 East Market Street   (14901)
Tel.: (607) 732-1928

Glens Falls
Planned Parenthood of Washington, Warren & Saratoga
   Counties
43 Lincoln Avenue   (12801)
Tel.: (518) 792-5148

Huntington
  Planned Parenthood Center of North Suffolk
  48 Elm Street   (11743)
  Tel.: (516) HA 7-7154
Ithaca
  Planned Parenthood of Tompkins County
  First Presbyterian Church—DeWitt Park   (14850)
  Tel.: (607) 273-1513
Mineola
  Planned Parenthood of Nassau County
  70 Third Avenue   (11501)
  Tel.: (516) PI 6-3484
Mount Kisco
  Planned Parenthood of Northern Westchester
  359 East Main Street   (10549)
  Tel.: (914) MO 6-6026
Mount Vernon
  Planned Parenthood Center of Southern Westchester
  16 South Second Avenue   (10550)
  Tel.: (914) MO 8-7926
Newburgh
  Planned Parenthood Center of Orange County
  74 Ann Street   (12550)
  Tel.: (914) 562-5748
New York City
  Planned Parenthood of New York City
  300 Park Avenue South   (10010)
  Tel.: (212) 777-2002
  Margaret Sanger Research Bureau
  17 West 16th Street   (10011)
  Tel.: (212) WA 9-6200
Niagara Falls
  Niagara Association for Planned Parenthood

825 Main Street   (14301)
Tel.: (716) BU 2-4110

Patchogue
Planned Parenthood of East Suffolk
119 North Ocean Avenue   (11772)
Tel.: (516) GR 5-5705

Port Chester
Planned Parenthood Center of Eastern Westchester
225 Westchester Avenue   (10573)
Tel.: (914) WE 9-1020

Poughkeepsie
Planned Parenthood League of Dutchess County
54 Noxon Street   (12603)
Tel.: (914) GR 1-1540

Rochester
Planned Parenthood League of Rochester and Monroe
   County
38 Windsor Street   (14605)
Tel.: (716) 546-2595

Schenectady
Planned Parenthood League of Schenectady County
1222 Union Street   (12308)
Tel.: (518) FR 4-9624

Syracuse
Planned Parenthood Center of Syracuse, Inc.
618 South Crouse Avenue   (13210)
Tel.: (315) 475-4114

Utica
Planned Parenthood Association of the Mohawk Valley
1675 Bennett Street   (13502)
Tel.: (315) 724-4356

Watertown
Planned Parenthood of Northern New York

161 Stone Street   (13601)
Tel.: (315) 788-8065
West Nyack
Planned Parenthood of Rockland County
37 Village Square   (10994)
Tel.: (914) EL 8-1145
Yonkers
Hudson River Committee for Planned Parenthood
45 Warburton Avenue   (10701)
Tel.: (914) YO 5-1912

NORTH CAROLINA
Asheville
Planned Parenthood Association of Western North Carolina
P.O. Box 5641   (28803)
Tel.: (704) 684-4811

OHIO
Akron
Planned Parenthood Association of Summit County, Inc.
331 East Market Street   (44304)
Tel.: (216) 376-9121
Canton
Planned Parenthood of Stark County
Room 203—106 High Avenue N.W.   (44703)
Tel.: (216) 455-5444
Cincinnati
Planned Parenthood Association of Cincinnati
2406 Auburn Avenue   (45219)
Tel.: (513) 721-7635
Cleveland
Planned Parenthood of Cleveland, Inc.

2027 Cornell Road   (44106)
Tel.: (216) 721-4700

Columbus
Planned Parenthood Association of Columbus
208 East State Street   (43215)
Tel.: (614) 224-8423

Dayton
Planned Parenthood Association of Miami Valley
15 Van Buren Street   (45402)
Tel.: (513) 223-4191

Hamilton
Planned Parenthood Association of Butler County
305 Front Street   (45011)
Tel.: (513) 893-0451

Mansfield
Planned Parenthood Association of the Mansfield Area
419 Bowman Street   (44903)
Tel.: (419) 525-3075

Springfield
The Planned Parenthood Center
10½ West Columbia Street   (45502)
Tel.: (513) 325-7349

Toledo
Planned Parenthood League of Toledo
217-15th Street   (43624)
Tel.: (419) 241-5142

Youngstown
Planned Parenthood Association of Youngstown
125 West Commerce Street   (44503)
Tel.: (216) 746-5641

OKLAHOMA

Muskogee
Planned Parenthood Center of Muskogee County

530 South 34th Street (P.O. Box 1503)   (74401)
Tel.: (918) MU 7-4456
Norman
Planned Parenthood of Cleveland County
P.O. Box 787   (76069)
Tel.: (405) JE 4-4048
Oklahoma City
Planned Parenthood Association
1031 North East 11 Street   (73117)
Tel.: (405) CE 5-1791
Tulsa
Planned Parenthood Association of Tulsa
1615 East 12 Street   (74120)
Tel.: (918) LU 4-1351, Ext. 590

OREGON
Eugene
Planned Parenthood Association of Lane County
16 East Broadway   (97402)
Tel.: (503) 344-9411
Medford
Planned Parenthood of Jackson County
P.O. Box 485   (97501)
Tel.: (503) 664-1665
Portland
Planned Parenthood Association, Inc.
620 North East Broadway   (97232)
Tel.: (503) 287-1189

PENNSYLVANIA
Bristol
Planned Parenthood Association of Bucks County
Professional Center—Bath Road & Route 13   (19007)
Tel.: (215) 788-4121

Easton
   Planned Parenthood Center of Easton
   Box 203   (18042)
   Tel.: (215) 258-9331
East Stroudsburg
   Monroe County Planned Parenthood Association
   P.O. Box 76   (18301)
   Tel.: (717) 421-4000
Erie
   Planned Parenthood Association of Erie County
   231 State Street   (16505)
   Tel.: (814) 454-7675
Harrisburg
   Tri-County Planned Parenthood Association
   2036 North 5th Street   (17102)
   Tel.: (717) 234-2468
Lancaster
   Planned Parenthood of Lancaster
   630 Janet Avenue   (17601)
   Tel.: (717) 394-3575
Philadelphia
   Planned Parenthood Association of Southeastern Penn-
      sylvania
   1402 Spruce Street   (19102)
   Tel.: (215) KI 6-8888
Pittsburgh
   Planned Parenthood Center of Pittsburgh, Inc.
   526 Penn Avenue   (15222)
   Tel.: (412) AT 1-9502
Reading
   Planned Parenthood Center of Berks County
   48 South 4th Street   (19602)
   Tel.: (215) 376-8061

Scranton
  Planned Parenthood Organization of Lackawanna
    County
  316 North Washington Avenue   (18503)
  Tel.: (717) DI 4-2626
Sharon
  Shenango Valley Planned Parenthood Association
  Boyle Building—149 East State Street   (16146)
  Tel.: (412) 347-1402
West Chester
  Planned Parenthood of Chester County
  33 East Washington Street   (19380)
  Tel.: (215) 692-1770
Wilkes-Barre
  Planned Parenthood Association of Luzerne County
  Kirby Memorial Health Center   (18701)
  Tel.: (717) VA 2-6830
York
  Planned Parenthood Committee of York County
  120 South Duke Street   (17403)
  Tel.: (717) 843-7151

RHODE ISLAND
Providence
  Planned Parenthood of Rhode Island
  46 Aborn Street   (02903)
  Tel.: (401) GA 1-9620

SOUTH CAROLINA
Beaufort
  Planned Parenthood Association of Beaufort County
  P.O. Box 884   (29902)
  Tel.: (803) 524-3446

Camden
    Planned Parenthood of Kershaw County
    205 Professional Building   (29020)
    Tel.: (803) HE 2-8101

Columbia
    Planned Parenthood of Richland & Lexington Counties
    Community Services Center
    1845 Assembly Street   (29201)
    Tel.: (803) 253-7737 or 254-3125

TENNESSEE

Knoxville
    Planned Parenthood Association of Knox County
    114 Dameron Avenue   (37917)
    Tel.: (615) 523-1722

Memphis
    Planned Parenthood Association of Memphis
    810 Washington Avenue   (38105)
    Tel.: (901) 527-7979

Nashville
    Planned Parenthood Association of Nashville
    814 Church Street   (37203)
    Tel.: (615) 256-4269

Oak Ridge
    Planned Parenthood Association of the Southern
        Mountains
    P.O. Box 88 (37830)
    Tel.: (615) 483-0283

TEXAS

Amarillo
    Planned Parenthood Committee of the Panhandle
    2308 West 7th Street   (79106)
    Tel.: (806) 373-2762

Austin
Planned Parenthood Center of Austin
1300 Sabine Street   (78701)
Tel.: (512) GR 2-7311

Brownsville
Cameron County Planned Parenthood Association
138 Fort Brown   (78520)
Tel.: (512) LI 6-1048

Corpus Christi
South Texas Planned Parenthood Center
2558 Morgan Avenue   (78405)
Tel.: (512) TU 4-4352

Dallas
Planned Parenthood of Dallas
3620 Maple Avenue   (75219)
Tel.: (214) LA 1-3191

Eagle Pass
Planned Parenthood of Maverick County
315 Bliss-P.O. Box 1146   (78852)
Tel.: (512) PR 3-9338

El Paso
Planned Parenthood Center of El Paso
214 West Franklin Street   (79901)
Tel.: (915) 532-5572

Ft. Worth
Planned Parenthood Center of Ft. Worth
614 West First Street   (76102)
Tel.: (817) ED 2-5053

Houston
Planned Parenthood of Houston
3512 Travis Street   (77002)
Tel.: (713) JA 3-7419

Lockhart
Planned Parenthood of Caldwell County

P.O. Box 333   (78644)
Tel.: (512) EX 8-5412

Lubbock
Planned Parenthood Center of Lubbock
1108 10th Street   (79401)
Tel.: (806) PO 2-2956

Midland
Permian Basin Planned Parenthood Inc.
P.O. Box 12   (79701)
Tel.: (915) MU 3-3691

Mission
Planned Parenthood Association of Hidalgo County
P.O. Box 244   (78572)
Tel.: (512) JU 5-4575

Robstown
Planned Parenthood of Robstown
112 Main Street   (78380)
Tel.: (512) 4204

San Angelo
Planned Parenthood Center of San Angelo
122 West Second Street   (76901)
Tel.: (915) 655-3748

San Antonio
Planned Parenthood Center of San Antonio
106 Warren Street   (78212)
Tel.: (512) CA 7-0107

Waco
Planned Parenthood Center of Waco
1121 Ross Street   (76706)
Tel.: (817) PL 2-4801

VERMONT

Burlington
Planned Parenthood of Champlain County

161 Elmwood Avenue   (05401)
Tel.: (802) 862-9706

VIRGINIA

Norfolk
Planned Parenthood of Norfolk, Inc.
Norfolk Public Health Center—Room 231
401 Colley Avenue   (23507)
Tel.: (703) 625-5591

Richmond
Virginia League for Planned Parenthood
2009 Monument Avenue   (23220)
Tel.: (703) 358-4919

WASHINGTON

Seattle
Planned Parenthood Center of Seattle
202 - 16th Avenue, South   (98144)
Tel.: (206) 324-9948

Yakima
Planned Parenthood Association of Yakima County
1424 Summitview Avenue   (98902)
Tel.: (509) CH 8-3625

WEST VIRGINIA

Parkersburg
Planned Parenthood Association of Parkersburg
P.O. Box 5222, Vienna, W. Va.   (26101)
Tel.: (304) 295-5615

WISCONSIN

Milwaukee
Planned Parenthood Association of Milwaukee
536 West Wisconsin Avenue   (53203)
Tel.: (414) 271-8181

MATERNITY AND INFANT CARE PROJECTS

Some cities in the United States have special projects to promote the health of mothers and infants. Call your local health department or contact the "Project Director" at one of the addresses listed below to find out if there is such a project in your area or in what other ways they may be helpful to you. (For additional information see pages 39 and 40.)

ALABAMA

Birmingham
   Jefferson County Department of Health
   1912-8th Avenue, South   (35233)
Mobile
   Mobile County Board of Health   (36604)

ARKANSAS

Little Rock
   State Health Building   (72202)

CALIFORNIA

Berkeley
   Department of Public Health
   2121 McKinley Avenue   (94703)
Los Angeles
   Los Angeles County Health Department
   220 North Broadway   (90012)
San Francisco
   101 Grove Street   (94102)

COLORADO

Denver
   Denver Department of Health & Hospitals
   West 6th Avenue & Cherokee Street   (80204)

Englewood
Tri-County District Health Department
180 East Hampden Avenue   (80110)

CONNECTICUT
Hartford
Hartford Health Department
56 Coventry Street   (06112)

DISTRICT OF COLUMBIA
Washington, D.C.
D.C. Department of Public Health
601 Indiana Avenue, N.W.   (20001)

FLORIDA
Ft. Lauderdale
Broward County Health Department
2421 S.W. 6th Avenue   (33302)
Gainesville
Florida State Department of Health and Rehabilitative Services
412 N.W. 16th Avenue   (32601)
Miami
Dade County Department of Public Health
1390 N.W. 14th Avenue   (33125)
Orlando
Orange County Health Department
Box 3187
832 Central Boulevard   (32802)
West Palm Beach
Palm Beach County Health Department
Box 29   (33402)

GEORGIA

Atlanta
    Grady Memorial Hospital
    80 Butler Street, S.E.   (30303)
Augusta
    Richmond County Health Department
    1001 Bailie Drive   (30902)

HAWAII

Honolulu
    State Department of Health
    P.O. Box 3378   (96801)

IDAHO

Boise
    State Department of Health
    Statehouse   (83702)

ILLINOIS

Springfield
    Illinois Department of Public Health   (62706)

KENTUCKY

Frankfort
    275 Main Street   (40601)

MAINE

Augusta
    Department of Health and Welfare
    Statehouse   (04330)

MARYLAND

Baltimore
    211 West Lombard Street   (21202)

MASSACHUSETTS

Boston
State Department of Public Health
484 Tremont Street   (02116)

MICHIGAN

Lansing
P.O. Box 1258   (48914)

MINNESOTA

Minneapolis
Minneapolis Health Department
250 South 4th Street   (55415)
St. Paul
St. Paul-Ramsey Hospital
640 Jackson Street   (55101)

MISSISSIPPI

Jackson
University Medical Center   (39205)

MISSOURI

Clayton
St. Louis County Health Department
801 South Brentwood Boulevard   (63105)
St. Louis
1421 North Jefferson Avenue   (63106)

NEBRASKA

Omaha
University of Nebraska College of Medicine
42nd and Dewey   (68105)

NEVADA

Reno
Reno-Washoe Health Department
10 Kirman Avenue   (89502)

NEW JERSEY

Newark
Metropolitan Health District
1100 Raymond Boulevard   (07102)

NEW MEXICO

Albuquerque
University of New Mexico School
of Medicine   (87106)

NEW YORK

Buffalo
775 Main Street   (14203)
New York
40 Worth Street   (10013)

NORTH CAROLINA

Raleigh
State Board of Health
225 N. McDowell Street   (27602)

OHIO

Cincinnati
2515 Burnet Avenue   (45219)
Cleveland
Metropolitan General Hospital
3395 Scranton Road   (44109)

OREGON

Portland
Oregon State Board of Health
P.O. Box 231   (97207)

PENNSYLVANIA

Philadelphia
500 South Broad Street   (19146)
Pittsburgh
Allegheny County Health Department
3447 Forbes Avenue   (15213)

RHODE ISLAND

Providence
State Department of Health   (02903)

SOUTH CAROLINA

Charleston
Charleston County Health Department   (29401)
Greenville
Greenville County Health Department   (29602)

TEXAS

Houston
Houston Health Department
1114 North MacGregor   (77205)
Sherman
County Health Department
P.O. Box 1295   (75090)

VIRGINIA

Richmond
500 N. 10th Street   (23219)

WASHINGTON

Olympia
Division of Health Services
Public Health Building   (98502)

WEST VIRGINIA

Charleston
1800 E. Washington Street   (25305)

SUGGESTED READINGS

Guttmacher, Alan F., W. Best, and F. S. Jaffe, *Birth Control and Love* (New York: Macmillan, 1969).

Guttmacher, Alan F., *Pregnancy and Birth* (New York: Signet Books, 1962).

Havemann, Ernest, and the Editors of Time-Life Books, *Birth Control* (New York: Time, Inc., 1967).

Isaac, Rael Jean, with Joseph Spencer, legal consultant, *Adopting a Child Today* (New York: Harper and Row, 1965).

Lader, Lawrence, *Abortion* (Boston: Beacon Press, 1967).

Osofsky, Howard J., M.D., *The Pregnant Teen-Ager* (Springfield, Ill.: Charles C Thomas, 1968).

Spock, Benjamin, M.D., *Baby and Child Care* (New York: Pocket Books, 1968).

Thompson, Jean, *The House of Tomorrow* (New York: Harper and Row, 1967). This book is a sensitive diary account of a pregnant girl's experience in a wage home affiliated with a Salvation Army home.

INDEX

Abortion(s): 20, 47–56, 167; thera-peutic, 18, 51, 54; and rape, 25; referral, help by, 38, 185; de-fined, 48; kinds of, 48–50; spon-taneous, 49; self-induced, 49–50; suggestions for proceeding, 50–53; cost of, 52–54; illegal, 54–55; after the, 55–56; psychological repercussions, 56

Admission, time of: and maternity homes, 69

Adoption: 116–137; and early diag-nosis, 21; help by agencies, 37; and maternity homes, 65; and baby's father, 118; and married women, 118n; types of, 118–129; agency, 119–123; procedures for selecting adoptive parents, 122–123; independent, 123–127; rela-tive, 127–128; why people adopt, 129–130; standards, 130–132; hard-to-place babies, 133–135; single-parent placements, 134

Adoption Resource Exchange of North America: 134–135

Adoptive homes: availability of, 70, 128–129

Age: and maternity homes, 70–71

Agency adoption: 119–123

Aid to Families with Dependent Children: 175

Aid to the Unborn: 96

Alabama: Planned Parenthood af-filiates, 186; maternity and infant care projects, 209

Alaska: Planned Parenthood affili-ates, 186

Amusement: 109–111

Anesthesia: 153

Apartments: 89–91

Arizona: Planned Parenthood affili-ates, 186

Arkansas: maternity and infant care projects, 209

Baby: due date, 18–19; black mar-ket, 128; feelings toward, 143, 156; if you give up, 166–169; keeping, 170–184; supplies, 172–173

Baby's father: and money, 93; in-formation about, 99; and adop-tion, 118; and birth certificate, 160

Birth certificates: 159–161

Birth control: 1–10, 179; after abor-tion, 55–56; and maternity homes, 79; after delivery, 165–166

Black girls: 69, 88, 134, 145

Boarding houses: 87–88

Boston Children's Service, Mass.: 119

Boyfriends: 24–26; and single mother, 183

Breasts: 104

California: abortion law, 20; and venereal disease, 114; abortion referrals phone number, 185; Planned Parenthood affiliates, 187–188; maternity and infant care projects, 209

Caseworkers. See Social workers

Catholic Family Service: 148

Catholic maternity homes: 63

Childbirth: classes in, 111–113; nat-ural, 113; your condition after, 163–164

Child care: 176–177

Children's Home Society, Califor-nia: 119

Child support: suing for, 173–174

Child Welfare Department: 36–37, 91

Circumcisions: 159

Civil rights: 55

Clergy Consultation Service: 52, 55

Clergymen: help by, 41

Clinics: 103

Medical social worker: 147–148
Medical society: 178–179
Menstrual period: missing, 13; last (LMP), 18
Michigan: abortion referral phone number, 185; Planned Parenthood affiliates, 193–194; maternity and infant care projects, 212
Military dependents: 103
Minnesota: Planned Parenthood affiliates, 194; maternity and infant care projects, 212
Minority groups: 133–134
Miscarriage: 20, 48
Mississippi: 61; maternity and infant care project, 212
Missouri: Planned Parenthood affiliate, 194; maternity and infant care projects, 212
Money. *See* Costs; Financial resources
Montana: Planned Parenthood affiliate, 194–195
Mood shifts: 109
Morning-after treatment: 11–12
Mutual service homes: 66, 75, 85–87

Narcotics. *See* Drugs
Nausea: 14
Nebraska: Planned Parenthood affiliate, 195; maternity and infant care projects, 212
Nevada: 61; maternity and infant care projects, 212
New Hampshire: 61; Planned Parenthood affiliates, 195
New Jersey: abortion referral phone number, 185; Planned Parenthood affiliates, 195–196; maternity and infant care projects, 213
New Mexico: Planned Parenthood affiliates, 196–197; maternity and infant care projects, 213
New York (City): abortion referral phone number, 185
New York (State): abortion law, 20, 47; abortion referral phone

number, 185; Planned Parenthood affiliates, 197–200; maternity and infant care projects, 213
North Carolina: Planned Parenthood affiliate, 200; maternity and infant care projects, 213
Nurses: as counselors, 150

Ohio: abortion referral phone number, 185; Planned Parenthood affiliates, 200–201; maternity and infant care projects, 213
Oklahoma: Planned Parenthood affiliates, 201–202
Oregon: Planned Parenthood affiliates, 202; maternity and infant care projects, 213
Orphanages: 135

Parents: 26–29
Pediatricians: 158–159
Pelvic exam: 17
Pennsylvania: abortion referral phone number, 185; Planned Parenthood affiliates, 202–204; maternity and infant care projects, 214
Physical changes: 104–106
Physicians. *See* Doctors
Pill, The: 8–9, 56, 165
Planned Parenthood: 12, 55, 114; help by, 36; and abortion laws, 47; affiliates listed by state, 186–208
Poland: abortion in, 53
Pregnancy: how it begins, 1; diagnosis of, 11–22; early symptoms, 13–14; tests for, 14–18; when baby due, 18–19; concealing, 57, 166–169; and self-consciousness, 59; first and maternity homes, 69–70; physical changes, 104–106; complaints that women have, 105–106; danger signs, 106; feeling comfortable, 108–109; counseling, 138–139
Premature births: 102
Prenatal: care, 21; visit, first, 104